LARRY SANG'S

Chinese Astrology & Feng Shui Guide

2009

The Year of the Ox

With Lorraine Wilcox

Larry Sang's
The Year of the Ox
ASTROLOGY AND FENG SHUI GUIDE

Original Title:
Master Larry Sang's 2009 The Year of the Ox, Astrology and Feng Shui Guide

Published by: The American Feng Shui Institute
111 N. Atlantic Blvd, Suite 352
Monterey Park, CA 91754. U.S.A.
Email: fsinfo@amfengshui.com
www.amfengshui.com

Written by:
Master Larry Sang

Co-authored by:
Lorraine Wilcox

Layout by:
Afriany Simbolon

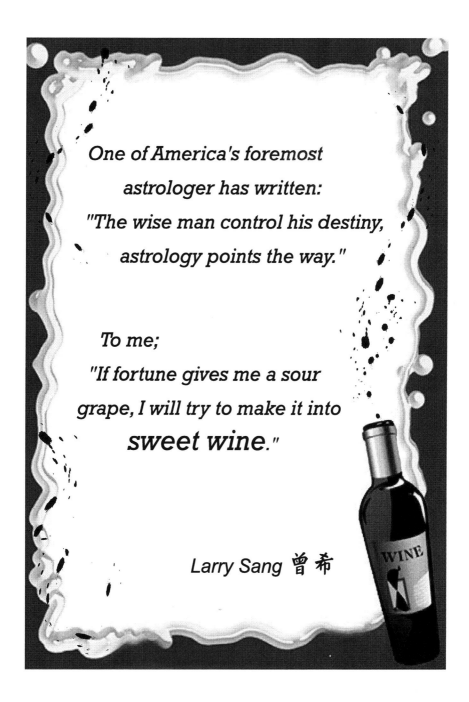

One of America's foremost astrologer has written:
"The wise man control his destiny, astrology points the way."

To me;
"If fortune gives me a sour grape, I will try to make it into **sweet wine.***"*

Larry Sang 曾希

3

Please Read This Information

This book provides information regarding the subject matter covered. The authors are not engaged in rendering legal, medical or other professional advice. If you need medical or legal advice, a competent professional should be contacted. Chinese Astrology and Feng Shui are not get-rich-quick or cure-all schemes. Changes in your life will happen as fast as you are ready for them. Be patient in your study of Chinese Astrology and Feng Shui.

The authors have tried to make this book as complete and accurate as possible. However, there may be typographical or content mistakes. Use this book as a general guide in your study of Chinese Astrology and Feng Shui

This book was written to educate and entertain. The authors, distributors and the American Feng Shui Institute shall have neither liability nor responsibility to any person with respect to any loss or damage caused, or alleged to be caused by this book.

The following pages of predictions will help you understand trends as they develop through the coming year. Please keep in mind that they are somewhat general because other stellar influences are operative, according to the month, date and exact minute of your birth. Unfortunately, we cannot deal with each person individually in this book.

Table of Contents

To live
in the simplest way.
Don't let complex thoughts
destroy the sweet life.

以最簡單的方式
生活，
不可讓複雜思想
破壞
生活的甜美。

Larry Sang 曾希

6

How to find your Animal Sign

In order to find your correct animal sign, as well as understand why the Chinese calendar begins in February, and not January, it is important to have a little understanding of the two different Chinese calendars. As with most things Chinese, we look at the Yin and Yang. In Chinese timekeeping, there is a Yin calendar (lunar calendar) and a Yang calendar (solar calendar).

The Lunar Calendar

The Lunar Calendar is perhaps the best known and most popular of the two. Chinese Lunar New Year is frequently celebrated with a lot of pageantry. It is used in one type of Chinese astrology called Zi Wei Dou Shu, and also in Yi-Jing calculations.

The Solar Calendar

The Solar calendar is less well known. The early Chinese meteorologists attempted to gain insight into the cycles of the seasons. From this study, they developed the Solar calendar. This calendar is used in the form of Chinese Astrology called Four Pillars, as well as in Feng Shui. The Chinese were very accurate in their studies. Without computers, and using only observations, they mapped a solar year of 365 days. They missed the actual timing of a year by only 14 minutes and 12 seconds.

The solar year is divided into 24 solar terms. Each lasts about fifteen days. Spring Begins (lichun) is the name of the first day of spring, and the first solar term. It is exactly midway between the winter solstice and the spring equinox. This is why it always falls on February 4th or 5th. We begin the five elements with wood, so the Chinese New Year begins with a wood month, whether in the Lunar or the Solar calendar. These concepts are derived from the Yi-Jing.

How to find your Animal Sign

To find your animal sign, start with your birth date. If it is before February 4th (Spring Begins), use the prior year for the Chinese calendar. If it is after February 4th, then use the same birth year. If it is on February 4th, then you need the time of the birth to accurately determine the birth animal. This information is contained in the Chinese Ten-Thousand Year Calendar. (The American Feng Shui Institute has one available as an ebook at www.amfengshui.com) In the following pages, the birth years are listed for each animal, but remember, if your birthday is before February 4th, use the previous year to determine the animal.

The Twelve Animals

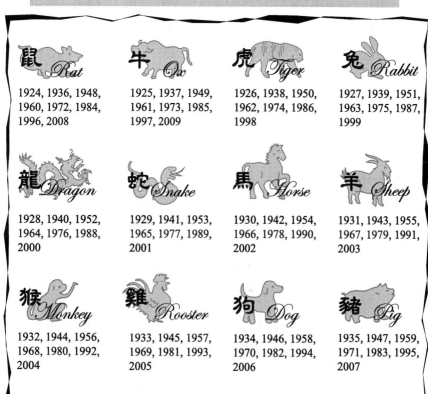

鼠 Rat
1924, 1936, 1948, 1960, 1972, 1984, 1996, 2008

牛 Ox
1925, 1937, 1949, 1961, 1973, 1985, 1997, 2009

虎 Tiger
1926, 1938, 1950, 1962, 1974, 1986, 1998

兔 Rabbit
1927, 1939, 1951, 1963, 1975, 1987, 1999

龍 Dragon
1928, 1940, 1952, 1964, 1976, 1988, 2000

蛇 Snake
1929, 1941, 1953, 1965, 1977, 1989, 2001

馬 Horse
1930, 1942, 1954, 1966, 1978, 1990, 2002

羊 Sheep
1931, 1943, 1955, 1967, 1979, 1991, 2003

猴 Monkey
1932, 1944, 1956, 1968, 1980, 1992, 2004

雞 Rooster
1933, 1945, 1957, 1969, 1981, 1993, 2005

狗 Dog
1934, 1946, 1958, 1970, 1982, 1994, 2006

豬 Pig
1935, 1947, 1959, 1971, 1983, 1995, 2007

Fortunes of the 12 Animals

The Ox

1925, 1937, 1949, 1961, 1973, 1985, 1997, 2009

Note: The New Year begins February 4ᵗʰ

After an auspicious year in 2008, it will be a challenging year for the Ox in 2009. Where career and jobs are concerned, the Ox will encounter a great deal of pressure and competition. With the Hua Gai star in Ming Palace, this will be a significant year in education for the Ox, with some important work projects and exams, as well as for choosing a subject to specialize in. The best time for you to proceed with your ambition is in the spring and summer. Money prospects are average. Income is slow and out-go is fast; therefore playing safe is the best policy. If you take an active stance, like going on overseas working trips or even vacation, avoid disputes with others while in foreign lands. Otherwise you may suffer financial losses or be hit by a lawsuit. Health-wise, there are no life-threatening illnesses. Beware of traffic accidents or injuries from sharp objects. Those who were born in 1961 may encounter problems with the eyes or heart. Your love life is not as colorful as last year. Though you may date fairly often, it is difficult to differentiate a sincere relationship from one that is not, so it will be quite a while before you find true love. Married couples will be emotional, hot and cold, and easily aroused to argue and lose control.

Your Benefactor is: Rooster
(1933, 1945, 1957, 1969, 1981, 1993, 2005)

12 Month Outlook For The Ox

Solar Month	Comments
1st Month Feb 4th - Mar 4th	Luck is normal. Not too much excitement nor too many obstacles.
2nd Month Mar 5th - Apr 4th	This is a relatively favorable month for relationships.
3rd Month Apr 5th - May 4th	Things are uncertain; knocks and bumps lie ahead.
4th Month May 5th - Jun 4th	Be conservative. Don't be aggressive or make decisions in a hurry.
5th Month Jun 5th - July 6th	Good in money luck. You may be bothered by backstabbers.
6th Month July 7th - Aug 6th	Money and peach blossom luck are strong. There is a sign of small consuming; budget wisely.
7th Month Aug 7th - Sept 6th	A big consuming star shines above; don't be greedy about money matters beyond your capability.
8th Month Sept 7th - Oct 7th	Auspicious stars shine above, good in all aspects.
9th Month Oct 8th - Nov 6th	Good time to develop something new; things will be achieved in the right place and time.
10th Month Nov 7th - Dec 6th	There is a sign of gossip. Say less and be humble.
11th Month Dec 7th - Jan 4th	Time for venturing overseas.
12th Month Jan 5th - Feb 3rd	The Tian Yi auspicious star may bring you a benefactor during social activities.

The Tiger

1926, 1938, 1950, 1962, 1974, 1986, 1998

Note: The New Year begins February 4th

The Ox year holds good fortune for the male Tiger and a mixed fortune for the female Tiger. There will be ample opportunities for male Tigers who are salaried workers to impress their bosses, especially in the spring and summer. Trying a career switch will bring about good results. For the self-employed who intend to go into a partnership, it is best to approach people born in the Monkey or Dog year. Money prospects are average. The prospects of female Tigers are encouraging for work matters, but she needs to take care when dealing with finances. In 2009, there could be many temptations to spend and it would certainly be in her interests to watch her money going out; otherwise this could exceed expectations. This is especially important at the end of the year, which is usually more expensive. In health, the physical discomfort you feel is caused by your moodiness due to the Mei Qi star in Ming Palace. For male Tigers, this is a good year for romance, and the best time to get married is in the summer. For the unattached female, take note: The prospects are mixed between sweet and sour. It would be best to let any new friendship form steadily, rather than rush into a hasty commitment. For the married female Tiger be careful of trouble from temptations outside the home.

Your Benefactor is: Dog
(1922, 1934, 1946, 1958, 1970, 1982, 1994, 2006)

12 Month Outlook For The Tiger

Solar Month	Comments
1st Month Feb 4th - Mar 4th	Enjoyable peach blossom; your mate or date knows just how to keep you smiling.
2nd Month Mar 5th - Apr 4th	There is a sign of anger or despair. Keep alert.
3rd Month Apr 5th - May 4th	Average luck. Advice from friends cannot be taken at face value. Your usual good judgment is at a low.
4th Month May 5th - Jun 4th	Good luck is predicted in money matters! Substantial gain can be expected.
5th Month Jun 5th - July 6th	Not a beneficial time for going out late at midnight. Be cautious of robbery.
6th Month July 7th - Aug 6th	Expenses for the month are uncertain. Do not be a guarantor. Trust nobody.
7th Month Aug 7th - Sept 6th	The most rewarding month this year; there is something good to celebrate!
8th Month Sept 7th - Oct 7th	Auspicious luck. Things are to your satisfaction.
9th Month Oct 8th - Nov 6th	There is a sign of conflict. Watch out for backstabbers. Silence is gold.
10th Month Nov 7th - Dec 6th	Busy month. Stress and tension could be higher than usual.
11th Month Dec 7th - Jan 4th	Focus on your health to prevent illness. Avoid overworking and relax more.
12th Month Jan 5th - Feb 3rd	There are small gains and big losses. Any new plan for the future requires care and consideration.

The Rabbit

1927, 1939, 1951, 1963, 1975, 1987, 1999

Note: The New Year begins February 4ᵗʰ

2009 will be a tricky year for the Rabbit. It won't necessarily be smooth or rough. Although parts of the year will go well, there are other elements that could cause problems. One of the areas of concern is the Rabbit's relations with others, and he must exercise great care with this. In particular, the Rabbit should make sure his attitude does not bring him into conflict with others and in that way jeopardize some of the good relationships he has built up. Two of the most inauspicious stars are tangling in Ming Palace, so be on guard in whatever you do, especially when signing documents. Keep your emotions aside when communicating with people and avoid acting as a guarantor for others. Career and money luck alternate between being auspicious and inauspicious. Salaried workers should act within the confines of their abilities and try not to over estimate themselves. Your health will generally be good and there are no signs of major illnesses. In the spring and summer, an aged family member may fall ill. Avoid visiting hospitals or attending funerals. Romance is not smooth this year. Rabbits born in 1975 need to be particularly cautious of entanglement in a disastrous romance. Married couples will be emotional, and frequent quarrels may lead to separation.

Your Benefactor is: Dragon
(1928, 1940, 1952, 1964, 1976, 1988, 2000)

12 Month Outlook For The Rabbit

Solar Month	Comments
1st Month Feb 4th - Mar 4th	Luck is average. You may frequently feel unwell or moody for no reason.
2nd Month Mar 5th - Apr 4th	Be satisfied with small gains; don't expect too much.
3rd Month Apr 5th - May 4th	Things are average to good. Be cautious of backstabbers.
4th Month May 5th - Jun 4th	Money prospects are at their best. Make use of it.
5th Month Jun 5th - July 6th	Keep on high alert. There is a sign of financial loss or bleeding.
6th Month July 7th - Aug 6th	Auspicious luck. Conditions are stimulating you to try something new.
7th Month Aug 7th - Sept 6th	Good opportunities come your way. Daily activities and surroundings are enjoyable.
8th Month Sept 7th - Oct 7th	This is a month of conflict and tension. Take a back seat and relax.
9th Month Oct 8th - Nov 6th	Better fortune in money luck for venturing overseas.
10th Month Nov 7th - Dec 6th	Take care of your health. Your mood is like a bouncing ball: high and low.
11th Month Dec 7th - Jan 4th	Signs of bleeding. Keep away from sharp objects.
12th Month Jan 5th - Feb 3rd	This is a relatively favorable month for relationships. Lots of social opportunities and peach blossom.

The Dragon

1928, 1940, 1952, 1964, 1976, 1988, 2000

Note: The New Year begins February 4th

This is a moderate year. The Dragon must persist in taking the initiative and be decisive to make gain in the Ox year. Otherwise, things will go downhill. The first season of the year finds you energetically pursuing a special field of education and taking care of business interests. This could involve acquiring new skills that will further your career. It is an unusually important time. Rapid advances can be made in business and career. You can achieve great progress this year. Be level-headed when commencing new work operations; do not leave things to luck. Money luck is unstable. Cast aside any thoughts of greed if you want to prevent financial mishaps. From June 5 through July 6, avoid financial speculation of any kind. Common health complaints for the Dragon this year are painful joints, rheumatism, and the likes. Take special care in the spring lest you dislocate a bone or joint. Where affairs of the heart are concerned, this is a good year for romance and marriage for females, while males may find themselves being neglected. Your most intimate personal relationship could be tense during the period from August 7 through September 6. Married couples will frequently fight over trivial matters. This may lead to someone walking away from home. Try to be more tolerant.

Your Benefactor is: Sheep
(1919, 1931, 1943, 1955, 1967, 1979, 1991, 2003)

12 Month Outlook For The Dragon

Solar Month	Comments
1st Month Feb 4th - Mar 4th	Average luck. Your family members may turn you from optimistic to gloomy with few hostile words.
2nd Month Mar 5th - Apr 4th	This is the time to lay a firm foundation for the future.
3rd Month Apr 5th - May 4th	Pleasant working relationships make this a good month to launch a new project.
4th Month May 5th - Jun 4th	Cast aside any thoughts of greed if you want to prevent financial mishaps.
5th Month Jun 5th - July 6th	Auspicious luck is foreseen in money matters.
6th Month July 7th - Aug 6th	Good aspects are seen in almost everything. Long-distance business ventures are promising.
7th Month Aug 7th - Sept 6th	Backstabbers are around. You will be easily caught in squabbles.
8th Month Sept 7th - Oct 7th	Luck is low. To be safe, do not visit sick people or attend funerals.
9th Month Oct 8th - Nov 6th	Relaxation is the top priority this month. Put aside all thought of work responsibilities.
10th Month Nov 7th - Dec 6th	Watch out for sharp objects which may cause bleeding.
11th Month Dec 7th - Jan 4th	Bath in the spring breeze! Things are so enjoyable.
12th Month Jan 5th - Feb 3rd	You feel busy physically and mentally.

The Snake

1929, 1941, 1953, 1965, 1977, 1989, 2001

Note: The New Year begins February 4th

2009 brings good tidings to the Snake. San Tai and the Golden Cabinet, a brilliant money star, combine qi in the Ming Palace, boosting the Snake's energy level and increasing the tempo of life. This enables the Snake to achieve much through tact and charm. Career and money prospects are abundant. It is also a good time to venture beyond the usual scope. You may encounter pressure and competition in work during the autumn, but luck is on your side. Though it is quite a good year, there are two inauspicious stars Guan Fu and Zhi Bei (lawsuits and backstabbing). Keep a low profile and be humble at all time. Sugarcoat your words and you should get all the cooperation you need. It is advisable for you to be on guard when signing a contract or document. Read all the fine print first and be sure you understand what it means. Think before doing anything that you know is not quite in accordance with the rules and regulations. Health-wise, apart from discomfort in your digestive system, there are no signs of major illness. The Snake's love relationship alternates between sweet and bitter this year. People around you may give you endless trouble and gossip. Though you may find a life partner, your relationship with him or her is fraught with frustration and difficulties. Married Snakes have a tendency to get involved in a short term romance.

Your Benefactor is: Monkey
(1920, 1932, 1944, 1956, 1968, 1980, 1992, 2004)

12 Month Outlook For The Snake

Solar Month	Comments
1st Month Feb 4th - Mar 4th	Things go well in money and career. There is a sign of gossip. Say less and be humble.
2nd Month Mar 5th - Apr 4th	Things are pleasurable! Enjoy the happy moods.
3rd Month Apr 5th - May 4th	A month of conflict. To avoid a financial mishap, do not depend on anyone.
4th Month May 5th - Jun 4th	Luck is noticeably moving upward. A long distance vacation may receive unexpected benefit.
5th Month Jun 5th - July 6th	Auspicious stars are gathering together. Matters turn out well in nearly all aspects.
6th Month July 7th - Aug 6th	Avoid anything secretive or underhanded.
7th Month Aug 7th - Sept 6th	Keep all moves simple and straightforward so that no one can accuse you of deception.
8th Month Sept 7th - Oct 7th	Any ongoing negotiations should be put on hold until conditions improve.
9th Month Oct 8th - Nov 6th	There is danger of losing a valued associate. Respond to a request whether you agree or disagree.
10th Month Nov 7th - Dec 6th	Things are uncertain. A wait and see attitude is the best policy.
11th Month Dec 7th - Jan 4th	Guard against back strain; don't lift a heavy load alone.
12th Month Jan 5th - Feb 3rd	Conditions are easygoing and comfortable.

The Horse

1918, 1930, 1942, 1954, 1966, 1978, 1990, 2002

Note: The New Year begins February 4th

This is a mixed year for the Horse, alternating between good and bad. Money comes and money goes. Failure comes as easily as success. The first six months of the Ox year are full of gain for the Horse. However, obstacles will start appearing after July. You need to save up to prepare for uncertainties during the rest of the year. Be on guard in whatever you do from autumn onward. Mental power is good but physical energy is in short supply. Put aside tasks requiring strength and concentrate on intellectual pursuits. There are signs of financial mishap and conflict with others in September. Keep your cool in whatever you do or you will mess things up. Come December, the Horse's luck will deteriorate even more; the only way to overcome the crisis is to be tolerant and be on your guard. Health-wise, you may suffer from allergies and minor respiratory ailments. It is advisable for you to take more rest. Romantic encounters are abundant and love relationships progress faster than expected. However, for the single Horse, if you want results, you must take the initiative. Married Horses will find it easy to have a third party intruder in their relationship. It is especially true for Horses born in 1966 and 1954. It is foreseen that a new relationship will show up for divorced Horses.

Your Benefactor is: Tiger
(1926, 1938, 1950, 1962, 1974, 1986, 1998)

12 Month Outlook For The Horse

Solar Month	C o m m e n t s
1st Month Feb 4th - Mar 4th	Sunny skies! Lots of social opportunities due to strong peach blossom luck.
2nd Month Mar 5th - Apr 4th	Watch out for cash-flow problems. Budget wisely.
3rd Month Apr 5th - May 4th	Strong in money luck. Work hard and focus on your target; the results will be as planned.
4th Month May 5th - Jun 4th	Auspicious luck. The plans and efforts you extend will be in rewarded in future.
5th Month Jun 5th - July 6th	Good and bad mixed. Double check all your work.
6th Month July 7th - Aug 6th	Average luck. Distant business ventures are promising.
7th Month Aug 7th - Sept 6th	Watch out for some illness or the flu.
8th Month Sept 7th - Oct 7th	Luck is low - advice about risky investment is untrustworthy.
9th Month Oct 8th - Nov 6th	Average luck. This is a good month to get married.
10th Month Nov 7th - Dec 6th	Be conservative. Things are unstable and uncertain.
11th Month Dec 7th - Jan 4th	This month can bring conflict and tension. Try to avoid people who aggravate you.
12th Month Jan 5th - Feb 3rd	Life moves upward. Daily activities and surroundings are easier than usual to handle.

The Sheep

1931, 1943, 1955, 1967, 1979, 1991, 2003

Note: The New Year begins February 4ᵗʰ

The Sheep is in conflict with the Ox, so it will be a year of challenge and it will also be an unstable time of floating and sinking. With the Da Hao star in Ming Palace, don't expect windfalls; avoid gambling or indulging in financial speculation. The beginning of the year possibly finds you involved with personal affairs, including the fulfillment of a financial obligation. A financial matter needs attention during the spring. You are vulnerable to accidents while traveling. Be extra cautious around vehicles of all kinds. Drive defensively and be sure to use your seat belt. But if you are a Sheep born in 1979, or born in the twelfth month (around January 6 to February 3), you hold a different fortune. You can expect considerable rewards in career. Where health is concerned, you need plenty of rest to overcome mental exhaustion. Other health complaints this year are neurasthenia and ailments of the circulatory system. It will be a year of hits and misses for the Sheep where romance is concerned. Though romantic encounters may lead to marriage, the Sheep will be quite emotional and easily fight with a loved one over trivial matters. Try your best not to nitpick or argue, otherwise, it may lead to separation. Those who are married should spend less time with their spouses to prevent frequent squabbles.

Your Benefactor is: Horse
(1930, 1942, 1954, 1966, 1978, 1990, 2002)

12 Month Outlook For The Sheep

Solar Month	Comments
1st Month Feb 4th - Mar 4th	Be on high alert for signs of overspending or financial loss.
2nd Month Mar 5th - Apr 4th	This is a rewarding month for both relationships and business. A good time to develop something new.
3rd Month Apr 5th - May 4th	Money luck is at its best! Plans and effort you extend will be rewarded.
4th Month May 5th - Jun 4th	Watch out for injuries or cuts.
5th Month Jun 5th - July 6th	Life is busy. Stress will be higher than usual.
6th Month July 7th - Aug 6th	Tian Yi Benefactor star is shinning above; an unexpected good surprise will come.
7th Month Aug 7th - Sept 6th	You will experience tense relationships with people.
8th Month Sept 7th - Oct 7th	For males, career and love are both happy, but they are frustrating for females.
9th Month Oct 8th - Nov 6th	A month filled with depression and frustration. Restrain yourself from any type of argument or fight.
10th Month Nov 7th - Dec 6th	Say less and be humble. There are signs that gossip will tangle things up.
11th Month Dec 7th - Jan 4th	Luck is smooth. Working hard will enable you strive for the best results.
12th Month Jan 5th - Feb 3rd	Romantic luck is strong and enjoyable.

The Monkey

1920, 1932, 1944, 1956, 1968, 1980, 1992, 2004

Note: The New Year begins February 4th

Last year the Monkey's luck was average. Not much excitement nor many obstacles. In the Ox year, things will be quite different. Auspicious stars like Zi Wei, Long De and Tian Xi gather in Ming Palace, enabling the Monkey to have a year of smooth sailing. Substantial rewards can be expected where career and money are concerned. The best time for you to proceed with your ambition is in spring. However, the inauspicious stars Guan Fu and Sudden Failure also mix in Ming Palace; even though your luck is extremely good, do not use underhanded ways or take short cuts to make money. If you do, you may lose everything and even worse, it may get you into trouble with the law. Those born in the sixth month (around July 7 to August 6) should be extra cautious of getting into trouble with the law over signing documents. Health-wise, avoid overworking. Common complaints are headaches and insomnia. Tian Xi celebration star shines high above, so the Monkey will have no trouble finding a prospective spouse. A fruitful relationship will come your way this autumn. Even feuding couples will kiss and make up. Married couples may have juniors to join in their love life. Those born in the sixth month (around July 7 to August 6) should stay way from liquor and undesirable liaisons.

Your Benefactor is: Rabbit
(1927, 1939, 1951, 1963, 1975, 1987, 1999)

12 Month Outlook For The Monkey

Solar Month	Comments
1st Month Feb 4th - Mar 4th	A rewarding month. Most things are to your satisfaction.
2nd Month Mar 5th - Apr 4th	Good opportunities come your way. Invest more time in your work, and the gains will be bountiful.
3rd Month Apr 5th - May 4th	Avoid believing gossip currently around you.
4th Month May 5th - Jun 4th	Taking a business or vacation trip may produce unexpected rewards.
5th Month Jun 5th - July 6th	Pay attention to your health to prevent illness.
6th Month July 7th - Aug 6th	Be careful of sharp objects that can cause bleeding.
7th Month Aug 7th - Sept 6th	Auspicious time to offer or receive a marriage proposal!
8th Month Sept 7th - Oct 7th	Lots of confusion in dealing with things. Conflict arises easily.
9th Month Oct 8th - Nov 6th	Luck is mixed. Do not be rushed into a decision that will have far-reaching effects.
10th Month Nov 7th - Dec 6th	Money luck is strong. Things will go mostly as you wish.
11th Month Dec 7th - Jan 4th	Things emerge well. Romantic encounters are plenty and totally enjoyable!
12th Month Jan 5th - Feb 3rd	Be alert for signs of overspending and money loss.

The Rooster

1921, 1933, 1945, 1957, 1969, 1981, 1993, 2005

Note: The New Year begins February 4th

Again, the Ox year is auspicious for the Rooster after the extraordinary good fortune of 2008. The plans put into motion toward the end of last year are beginning to reap rewards for you in this year. A profitable investment opportunity will come your way in February. Career and money prospects are at their best from October 8 to November 6. However, expect setbacks and obstacles from August 7 to September 6. Be prepared for any contingency and you will go through the year without any major mishap. The salaried worker can look forward to a promotion or a change of environment in the mid-summer. For the self-employed, surprises throughout the year keep you on your toes and moving to a fast beat. Though money prospects are good, your expenditures will also rise correspondingly. Stick to what is simple and straight forward. It is not smart to become involved in any sort of plot. Health wise, you will experience discomfort in your digestive system and toothaches. This is a good year for courting couples to get married. Those who are single may meet their ideal life partners. A fruitful relationship awaits you this year. July 7 through August 6 and December 7 through January and into February 4 of 2010 are the best time to get married. Married Roosters born in 1981 should avoid getting involved in a love triangle.

Your Benefactor is: Snake
(1929, 1941, 1953, 1965, 1977, 1989, 2001)

12 Month Outlook For The Rooster

Solar Month	Comments
1st Month Feb 4th - Mar 4th	Auspicious luck. Start the work-month with a plan of attack to help you achieve long-term goals.
2nd Month Mar 5th - Apr 4th	Good opportunities. Be ready to take advantage of a change.
3rd Month Apr 5th - May 4th	Life is busy. This is a favorable month for travel.
4th Month May 5th - Jun 4th	Some luck is foreseen in money matters.
5th Month Jun 5th - July 6th	Any cooperation that you require is yours for the asking.
6th Month July 7th - Aug 6th	An auspicious time to offer or receive a marriage proposal!
7th Month Aug 7th - Sept 6th	Double-check details that others have turned over to you; their thoroughness is in doubt.
8th Month Sept 7th - Oct 7th	Do not ignore talk of a possible lawsuit. Problems may arise.
9th Month Oct 8th - Nov 6th	Money and career luck are in good sight.
10th Month Nov 7th - Dec 6th	Luck is smooth sailing. Things will go mostly as you wish.
11th Month Dec 7th - Jan 4th	Be alert for signs of overspending and money loss.
12th Month Jan 5th - Feb 3rd	Things emerge well. Romantic encounters are plenty, and everything is so enjoyable!

The Dog

1922, 1934, 1946, 1958, 1970, 1982, 1994, 2006

Note: The New Year begins February 4th

With the auspicious stars Tian De and Fu Xing inside the Ming Palace, the Dog will have relatively good fortune in the Ox year. Career and money prospects are looking up. However, you must be on guard whatever you do and be wary of vile characters around you. Since your good fortune is not consistent, it runs quite differently from one month to another. Under the influence of Xing Chong, a star of contention, there is a strong sign of conflict with others. You are prone to temper outbursts and tend to get angry over the most trivial matter. Even worse, you may even get hit by lawsuits. Keep your emotions under tight control in all situations and you will go through the year without any mishap. The self-employed will have opportunities for further development. A promotion and pay raise will come the way of salaried workers. You will be relative healthy, but watch out for the flu and migraines. Those born in 1994 should refrain from climbing to high places to prevent sprains and fractures. Where affairs of the heart are concerned, you will meet a number of setbacks due to the Gua Su (sleep alone) star entering into your Ming Palace, so it is natural for you to feel empty and lonely. For married couples, disputes with your loved one will occur frequently. Try to be more understanding towards each other.

Your Benefactor is: Ox
(1925, 1937, 1949, 1961, 1973, 1985, 1997, 2009)

12 Month Outlook For The Dog

Solar Month	Comments
1st Month Feb 4th - Mar 4th	Tense relationships with people. Conflicts easily arise.
2nd Month Mar 5th - Apr 4th	It is beneficial to travel and have sunshine on you.
3rd Month Apr 5th - May 4th	This is a relatively uneasy month: moody and lonely.
4th Month May 5th - Jun 4th	Be conservative. Luck is low.
5th Month Jun 5th - July 6th	Good in money luck for the self-employed, and a pay raise may come to salaried workers.
6th Month July 7th - Aug 6th	Keep on high alert. Sweet things can turn sour.
7th Month Aug 7th - Sept 6th	Gossip will bother you. But a benefactor may show up.
8th Month Sept 7th - Oct 7th	Luck is average. Watch out for the flu or cuts.
9th Month Oct 8th - Nov 6th	Money luck is at its best. You may discover a new source of income.
10th Month Nov 7th - Dec 6th	Be conservative. This is quite an uneventful month for both career and money luck.
11th Month Dec 7th - Jan 4th	Very strong good luck. Put more effort into reaching your target. The gains are bountiful.
12th Month Jan 5th - Feb 3rd	This month holds good fortune for proceeding with personal plans.

The Pig

1923, 1935, 1947, 1959, 1971, 1983, 1995, 2007

Note: The New Year begins February 4th

Things will be relatively peaceful for the Pig this year except for during June 5 through July 6 when there are hidden danger signs of bleeding and family members getting hit by illness. With the presence of Yi Ma, your daily life will keep busy, and it is quite beneficial for venturing overseas. Take an active stance, for example going on an overseas working trip, for it will put you in contact with some people who will benefit you and help advance your career. For the self-employed, the busier the better they are. For salaried workers, a job switch will bring good results. There are two inauspicious stars mixed in Ming Palace, one for mourning and another one brings sickness and money loss. However, financial losses can be prevented with careful judgment and budgeting wisely. Health-wise, it is possible that you may experience some disturbing symptoms, especially from October 8 through November 6, so be sure to see a doctor. Chances are there's nothing really wrong – but if there is, the quicker you get any necessary treatment, the better. With Yi Ma influencing your romance, there is a lot of vibration in the single Pig's love life. You should stay rational and refrain from being overly busy in the relationship. For married couples, your partner will complain that you don't spend enough time with him or her, and that's actually true.

Your Benefactor is: Rat
(1924, 1936, 1948, 1960, 1972, 1984, 1996, 2008)

12 Month Outlook For The Pig

Solar Month	Comments
1st Month Feb 4th - Mar 4th	Luck is average to good. Life is busy.
2nd Month Mar 5th - Apr 4th	You feel quite flabby and dyspeptic, so avoid doing yourself harm by being overly busy.
3rd Month Apr 5th - May 4th	Energy is low. You can easily become inattentive and moody.
4th Month May 5th - Jun 4th	This is an enjoyable month for romance. An interesting relationship may lead to marriage.
5th Month Jun 5th - July 6th	Obligations to a friend or to a family member could be a big drain on your finances.
6th Month July 7th - Aug 6th	There are hidden danger signs of bleeding and family members getting hit by illness.
7th Month Aug 7th - Sept 6th	This month is blessed. There are lots of opportunities waiting at the front door.
8th Month Sept 7th - Oct 7th	Good in money aspects, so take advantage of this month to get the financial rewards you deserve.
9th Month Oct 8th - Nov 6th	If you experience disturbing symptoms, be sure to see a doctor for a physical check up.
10th Month Nov 7th - Dec 6th	Tian Xi star shines above; celebration enters your door. The whole month passes by happily.
11th Month Dec 7th - Jan 4th	There is a lot of emphasis on the social scene and various vacation-type enjoyments this month.
12th Month Jan 5th - Feb 3rd	Average luck. You feel busy physically and mentally.

The Rat

1924, 1936, 1948, 1960, 1972, 1984, 1996, 2008

Note: The New Year begins February 4th

With Sui He and Tian Yi shining high above, the Ox year is blessed. It generally indicates that financial interests are accented at this time. This year's communications should include a few that make you very happy. They may concern anything from a much desired social invitation, a glamorous travel opportunity, good news concerning a business deal or a wage increase, and/or celebrating news of getting married or having a baby. Strong money luck and substantial gains can be expected by taking a long distance journey between August 7 and September 6. However, in the following month from September 7 through October 7, there are signs of financial mishap. You are likely to incur unnecessary expenditures. There is a need to budget wisely and keep expenses under control. Be conservative and on guard in career or job changes. It is not an appropriate time to make changes. Hold your ground unless convinced that changes are necessary. Health-wise, under the influence of Bing Fu (sickness) star, you must be careful of being attacked by sudden illness. Therefore, you should stay away from places such as hospitals where contagious diseases can be found. Romance will be fruitful because of the Sui He star. There is a great opportunity for marriage. Married Rat relationships will be relatively harmonious through the year.

Your Benefactor is: Pig
(1923, 1935, 1947, 1959, 1971, 1983, 1995, 2007)

12 Month Outlook For The Rat

Solar Month	C o m m e n t s
1st Month Feb 4th - Mar 4th	Enjoyable! Things are flowing smoothly.
2nd Month Mar 5th - Apr 4th	Focus on your target and work hard. Results will be as planned.
3rd Month Apr 5th - May 4th	Romantic luck is strong. Things are pleasurable.
4th Month May 5th - Jun 4th	Exercise more. Stay away from places such as hospitals where contagious diseases occur.
5th Month Jun 5th - July 6th	Conditions are fortunate for your interests.
6th Month July 7th - Aug 6th	All personal relationships are easygoing. Good opportunities exist in your own backyard.
7th Month Aug 7th - Sept 6th	Substantial gains can be expected by taking a long distance journey.
8th Month Sept 7th - Oct 7th	A month of conflict. Put a stop to unnecessary overspending.
9th Month Oct 8th - Nov 6th	Luck is good. The gains will be rather significant from money you invest.
10th Month Nov 7th - Dec 6th	Auspicious stars smile on you. Don't let your good luck slip through your fingers.
11th Month Dec 7th - Jan 4th	Tense relationships with people. Gossip arises easily.
12th Month Jan 5th - Feb 3rd	Avoid excesses of any kind, such as eating, drinking, sporting, late night partying, or whatever.

The secret of success
is to have zeal
and
dare to take risks.

成功之道
乃在於
擁有熱誠
及敢于
冒險的精神。

Larry Sang 曾希

Li Ming

Table 1   Li Ming (Establish Fate): Step 1-Determine your Palace

Li Ming for 2009

This is another system for making annual predictions.

☆ First, use Table 1, based on your month and time of birth.

☆ Take the results of Table 1, and use them in Table 2, along with your year of birth, to find the palace of Li Ming for 2009.

☆ Once you know the palace of Li Ming, read the prediction that follows for that palace.

Birth Hour:	Jan 21 1st Month	Feb 19 2nd Month	Mar 20 3rd Month	Apr 20 4th Month	May 21 5th Month	June 21 6th Month	July 23 7th Month	Aug 23 8th Month	Sep 23 9th Month	Oct 23 10th Month	Nov 22 11th Month	Dec 22 12th Month
11p - 1 a	Mao	Yin	Chou	Zi	Hai	Xu	You	Shen	Wei	Wu	Si	Chen
1 - 3 a	Yin	Chou	Zi	Hai	Xu	You	Shen	Wei	Wu	Si	Chen	Mao
3 - 5 a	Chou	Zi	Hai	Xu	You	Shen	Wei	Wu	Si	Chen	Mao	Yin
5 - 7 a	Zi	Hai	Xu	You	Shen	Wei	Wu	Si	Chen	Mao	Yin	Chou
7 - 9 a	Hai	Xu	You	Shen	Wei	Wu	Si	Chen	Mao	Yin	Chou	Zi
9 -11a	Xu	You	Shen	Wei	Wu	Si	Chen	Mao	Yin	Chou	Zi	Hai
11a - 1p	You	Shen	Wei	Wu	Si	Chen	Mao	Yin	Chou	Zi	Hai	Xu
1 - 3 p	Shen	Wei	Wu	Si	Chen	Mao	Yin	Chou	Zi	Hai	Xu	You
3 - 5 p	Wei	Wu	Si	Chen	Mao	Yin	Chou	Zi	Hai	Xu	You	Shen
5 - 7 p	Wu	Si	Chen	Mao	Yin	Chou	Zi	Hai	Xu	You	Shen	Wei
7 - 9 p	Si	Chen	Mao	Yin	Chou	Zi	Hai	Xu	You	Shen	Wei	Wu
9 -11p	Chen	Mao	Yin	Chou	Zi	Hai	Xu	You	Shen	Wei	Wu	Si

Born After:

Notes: These months are different from the solar (Feng Shui/Four Pillars) months, and also are different from the lunar months. They begin on the *Qi* of the *Twenty-four Jieqi*. If born within a day of these month dates, please consult a *Ten-Thousand Year Calendar* to determine exactly which is your birth month in this system. It is not necessary for you to understand the Chinese terms in the tables. Just follow the tables to the correct palace for you.

Table 2 Li Ming (Establish Fate): Step 2-Palace for a Chou (Ox) Year
Li Ming for 2009

Birth Year:

Li Ming: ▶ / Birth Year: ▲	Rat Zi	Ox Chou	Tiger Yin	Rabbit Mao	Dragon Chen	Snake Si	Horse Wu	Sheep Wei	Monkey Shen	Rooster You	Dog Xu	Pig Hai
Zi	Hai	Zi	Chou	Yin	Mao	Chen	Si	Wu	Wei	Shen	You	Xu
Chou	Zi	Chou	Yin	Mao	Chen	Si	Wu	Wei	Shen	You	Xu	Hai
Yin	Chou	Yin	Mao	Chen	Si	Wu	Wei	Shen	You	Xu	Hai	Zi
Mao	Yin	Mao	Chen	Si	Wu	Wei	Shen	You	Xu	Hai	Zi	Chou
Chen	Mao	Chen	Si	Wu	Wei	Shen	You	Xu	Hai	Zi	Chou	Yin
Si	Chen	Si	Wu	Wei	Shen	You	Xu	Hai	Zi	Chou	Yin	Mao
Wu	Si	Wu	Wei	Shen	You	Xu	Hai	Zi	Chou	Yin	Mao	Chen
Wei	Wu	Wei	Shen	You	Xu	Hai	Zi	Chou	Yin	Mao	Chen	Si
Shen	Wei	Shen	You	Xu	Hai	Zi	Chou	Yin	Mao	Chen	Si	Wu
You	Shen	You	Xu	Hai	Zi	Chou	Yin	Mao	Chen	Si	Wu	Wei
Xu	You	Xu	Hai	Zi	Chou	Yin	Mao	Chen	Si	Wu	Wei	Shen
Hai	Xu	Hai	Zi	Chou	Yin	Mao	Chen	Si	Wu	Wei	Shen	You

Notes:

☆ Take the Palace of Li Ming, found in the Table 1, and compare it to the year of birth to find the palace for 2009, a Chou (Ox) year.

☆ Use January 21st as the beginning of the new year for finding the birth year. If the birth date falls within one day of January 21st, check in a *Ten-Thousand Year Calendar* to be sure. If the birth date is between January 1st and January 20th, consider the person as belonging to the previous year in this system.

☆ The predictions described below go from January 20th, 2009 until January 19th, 2010.

37

Li Ming Palace Reading

Z i

With Sui He and Tian Yi stars shining above, financial interests are accented at this time. This should include a few things that make you very happy. Strong money luck and substantial gains can be expected. Good news concerning a business deal or a wage increase, and celebratory news of getting married may come. Under the influence of Bing Fu star, be careful of being attacked by sudden illness. Stay away from places such as hospitals where contagious diseases occur.

Chou

A year of challenge and unstable conditions. Have realistic expectations or you will be disappointed. There is a strong possibility of a job-related move or career changes. With the Hua Gai star in Ming Palace, this will be a significant year for those still in school with good academic results. When taking an overseas business trip, elevate your alert level to avoid conflicts with others. You may suffer financial losses or be hit by a lawsuit. Beware of traffic accidents or injuries from sharp objects.

Y i n

There will be ample opportunities for salaried workers to receive raises. A career switch will bring about good results. Females need to take care when dealing with finances. There could be many temptations to watch out for; otherwise she could exceed her budget and get into trouble. Even though Hong Luan star is in Ming Palace, please take note: The prospects are mixed between sweet and sour. It is not wise to rush into a hasty commitment.

Mao

Not a year to be overly optimistic. Things beyond your control could suddenly change from sweet to sour. Due to two inauspicious stars tangling in Ming Palace, be on guard in whatever you do, especially when signing documents. You must exercise great care that your attitude does not bring conflict with others. Otherwise you could ruin good relationships built up in the past. Keep your emotions aside when communicating with people and avoid acting as a guarantor for others. Take care of elderly family members. Avoid visiting hospitals or attending funerals.

Chen

If Li Ming is here, you should persist in taking the initiative and be decisive in order to make substantial gains. Rapid advances can be made in business and career. The first season of the year finds you energetically pursuing a special field of education and taking care of business interests. Money luck is unstable. Cast aside any thoughts of greed if you want to prevent financial mishaps. There are signs of conflicts in relationships. Do not give rude criticism when you are feeling emotional.

Si

San Tai and Golden Cabinet combine in the Ming Palace to boost your energy level and increase the tempo of life. This is a good time to venture beyond the usual scope. However, there are also two inauspicious stars Guan Fu and Zhi Bei. It is advisable for you to be on guard when signing a contract or document. Think before doing anything that you know is not quite in accordance with the rules and regulations; otherwise, it is possible to tangle with legal matters.

Wu

This year alternates between good and bad. Failure comes as easily as success. An inauspicious Xiao Hao star is in Ming Palace, so money comes and money goes. You need to save up to prepare for uncertainties and increase of expenditures. Mental power is good but physical energy is in short supply. Put aside tasks requiring strength and concentrate on intellectual pursuits. Romantic encounters and love relationship progress faster than expected. It is foreseen that a new relationship will show up for the divorced.

Wei

Li Ming contains Da Hao and Sui Po, so it will be a challenging and unstable year. There is the possibility of a financial mishap related to business contracts or taking place within the family. Do not expect windfalls; avoid gambling or indulging in financial speculation. Fortunately, the Di Jie star may help cancel a lot of negative qi. Be extra cautious around vehicles of all kinds while traveling. Drive defensively and be sure to use your seat belt. Plenty of rest is needed to overcome mental exhaustion.

Shen Zi Wei, Long De, and Tian Xi are in Ming Palace, so a year of smooth sailing and substantial rewards can be expected. However, Guan Fu and Sudden Failure star also mix in the Ming; do not use underhanded ways or take short cuts to make money. Otherwise, you may lose everything or even worse, it may get you into trouble with the law because of Guan Fu. The celebration star Tian Xi may bring a new member to join your family; getting married or having a baby is likely.

You With many auspicious stars around, this year your income will rise and blessings will be received. It is predicted that the whole year is safe and sound. Salaried workers can look forward to a promotion or a change of environment. For the self-employed, surprises throughout the year keep you on your toes and keep you moving to a fast beat. Wen Chang star will bring good academic results for those still in school. However, be cautious; self-indulgence will bring the consumption of many small things.

Xu With Tian De and Fu Xing inside the Ming Palace, career and money prospects are looking up. However, your good fortune is not consistent: under the influence of Xing Chong, a star of contention, there is a strong sign of conflict with others. Be wary of vile characters around you. Keep your emotions under tight control in all situations. The self-employed will have opportunities for further development. A promotion and pay raise will come the way of salaried workers.

Hai With Li Ming here, things will be relatively peaceful. Because of the presence of Yi Ma, it is quite beneficial for venturing overseas. Take an active stance, like going on an overseas working trip; it will put you into contact with some beneficial people who will help advance your career. A job switch will bring good results for salaried workers. The Diao Ke star in Ming Palace is a sign of the possibility of wearing mourning clothes. Take more care of elderly members in family. Avoid visiting the sick and attending funerals.

Omens

Omens

In Chinese almanacs, there are often listings of predictions based on omens. We include a few below. Have fun with it and don't take it too seriously.

Omens from the Twitch of an Eye

Time	Eye	This is an omen of:
11pm-1am	left	Meeting a benefactor.
zi	right	Having a good meal.
1-3am	left	Having anxiety.
chou	right	Someone thinking about you.
3-5am	left	Someone coming from afar.
yin	right	A happy matter arriving.
5-7am	left	The coming of an important guest.
mao	right	Something peaceful, safe, and auspicious.
7-9am	left	A guest coming from afar.
chen	right	Injury or harm.
9-11am	left	Having a good meal.
si	right	Something inauspicious.
11am-1pm	left	Having a good meal.
wu	right	An inauspicious matter.
1-3pm	left	A lucky star.
wei	right	Good luck, but small.
3-5pm	left	Money coming.
shen	right	Someone thinking of you romantically.
5-7pm	left	A guest coming.
you	right	A guest arriving.
7-9pm	left	A guest arriving.
xu	right	A gathering or meeting.
9-11pm	left	A guest arriving.
hai	right	Gossip.

Correct for *Daylight Savings Time*, if in use (subtract one hour from the current time).

Omens from Hiccoughs	
Time	**This is an omen of:**
11pm-1am zi	A good meal and a happy dinner gathering.
1-3am chou	Someone missing you; a guest coming to seek your help.
3-5am yin	Someone missing you; a dining engagement.
5-7am mao	Wealth and happiness; someone coming to ask about a matter.
7-9am chen	A good meal; great good luck for everyone.
9-11am si	A lucky person coming to seek wealth.
11am-1pm wu	An important guest; someone wanting a dinner gathering.
1-3pm wei	Someone wanting a meal; lucky activities.
3-5pm shen	Nightmares; eating is not beneficial.
5-7pm you	Someone coming; someone asks about a matter.
7-9pm xu	Someone missing you; a meeting brings benefit.
9-11pm hai	Something frightens, but on the contrary, brings benefit.

Correct for *Daylight Savings Time*, if in use (subtract one hour from the current time).

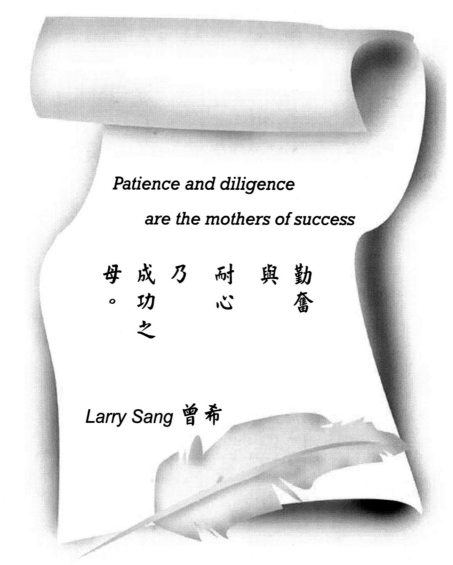

Patience and diligence

are the mothers of success

勤奮與耐心乃成功之母。

Larry Sang 曾希

44

The Yellow Emperor

The Yellow Emperor in the Four Seasons

黃帝四季詩

Spring

Autumn

Summer

Winter

There is a lifetime prediction commonly found in Chinese almanacs. Based on your season of birth, find your birth time.

The Yellow Emperor in the Four Seasons

		Season of Birth			
Time of Birth		Spring February 4th to May 4th	Summer May 5th to August 6th	Autumn August 7th to November 6th	Winter November 7th to February 3rd
Zi	11p-1a	head	low abdomen	shoulders	low abdomen
Chou	1-3a	chest	hands	hands	knees
Yin	3-5a	feet	feet	knees	chest
Mao	5-7a	shoulders	shoulders	chest	shoulders
Chen	7-9a	knees	knees	feet	feet
Si	9-11a	hands	hands	hands	head
Wu	11a-1p	low abdomen	head	shoulders	hands
Wei	1-3p	hands	chest	chest	knees
Shen	3-5p	feet	feet	low abdomen	chest
You	5-7p	shoulders	shoulders	knees	shoulders
Xu	7-9p	knees	knees	feet	feet
Hai	9-11p	chest	chest	head	hands

Correct birth time for Daylight Saving Time, if used at the time of birth. If you were born in the Southern Hemisphere, switch the autumn and spring dates, as well as the summer and winter dates.

The Yellow Emperor in the Four Seasons

Born on the Yellow Emperor's head means a lifetime of never having worries. Even petty people have riches and honor. Clothes and food naturally come around. Your position in society is elevated, and gentlemen are good at planning. Women go through life steadily and smoothly, marrying a talented and educated person.

Born on the Yellow Emperor's hands means business capital is sufficient. Going out, you meet a benefactor. Inside the home, you have everything. Your early years are very steady and smooth. You accumulate many possesions. Wealth comes from every direction. When old, it is in your hands.

Born on the Yellow Emperor's shoulders means a life of a million riches. You have wealth in your middle years. Children and grandchildren are plenty. Clothes and income at all times are good. In old age, you have fields in the village. Siblings are helpful. Your early life is bitter, but the later end is sweet.

Born on the Yellow Emperor's chest means clothes and food are naturally ample. Experts in the pen and the sword are around you. There is music, song, and dance. Middle age brings good clothes and food. Later years are happy and prosperous. Joy, utmost honor, prosperity, and increased longevity add more blessings.

Born on the Yellow Emperor's lower abdomen, you were treasured by your parents. In middle age, clothes and food are good. When old you obtain gold. The family reputation is changing a lot. You are a noble person. Children and grandchildren must newly shine. Cultured and bright, they advance a lot.

Born on the Yellow Emperor's knees means doing things is without benefit. In your early years, you toiled a lot, but did not lack clothes and food. Every day, you travel on the road; you cannot avoid running back and forth. Old age is smooth, with honor and prosperity, but in middle age, hard work is extreme.

Born on the Yellow Emperor's feet, practice moral teachings to avoid toil. A lifetime that is safe and sound, but unsuitable to reside in your ancestor's home. Women marry two husbands. Men have two wives. Search lonely mountain ranges. Leave your homeland to achieve good fortune.

Feng Shui

Feng Shui

Makes the Universe Work for You

We live in a universe that is filled with different energies. Our planet rotates on its axis, creating cycles of day and night. The earth also revolves around the sun in yearly cycles and is subject to various gravitational and magnetic fields. Our solar system is moving through space and is also subject to other forces in the universe.

These physical forces and many different time cycles affect us profoundly. The Chinese have spent centuries observing the effects of these forces, and learning how to better harmonize humans with their environment. This is the science and art of Feng Shui (Chinese geomancy).

Feng Shui uses observation, repeatable calculations and methodologies, and is based on the study of the environment, both inside and out of the house. Feng Shui can help you determine the best home to live in, which colors can enhance your home, the best bed positions for deep sleep, and how to change your business or home into a center of power. Feng Shui can help improve your health, your relationships and your prosperity. It is based on a complex calculation and observation of the environment, rather than a metaphysical reading relying on inspiration or intuition.

The American Feng Shui Institute publishes the annual Chinese Astrology and Feng Shui Guide so that both the Feng Shui professional and layperson can benefit from the knowledge of the incoming energy cycles and their influences. With this knowledge, one can adjust their environment to make it as harmonious as possible for the year 2009.

The following sections contain the energy patterns for 2009 with an analysis and remedy for each of the eight directions. For the nonprofessional, there is a section on how to prepare your home for this reading. Please note that Feng Shui is a deep and complex science that requires many years to master. Preparing your home to receive the annual energy is one aspect that anyone can apply. A professional reading is recommended to anyone who wishes to receive the greatest benefits possible that Feng Shui can bring.

Preparing your home for a Feng Shui Reading

The Floor Plan

The first requirement for preparing your home for a Feng Shui annual reading is to create a proportional floor plan. This plan can be hand drawn or be the original building plans, as long as the plan is proportionally correct. It is not necessary to draw in all your furniture except perhaps noting your bed and desk. It is important that you indicate where all window and door openings are.

**Example A
Floor plan**

**Example B
Floor plan**

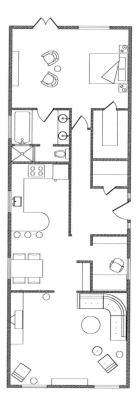

Gridding The Floor Plan

Once you have your floor plan drawn, you then overlay a 9- square grid. This grid is proportional to the floor plan. If it were a long and narrow house, so would the grid be long and narrow. You want to divide the floor plan into equal thirds both top to bottom and left to right as shown below:

**Example A
with grid**

**Example B
with grid**

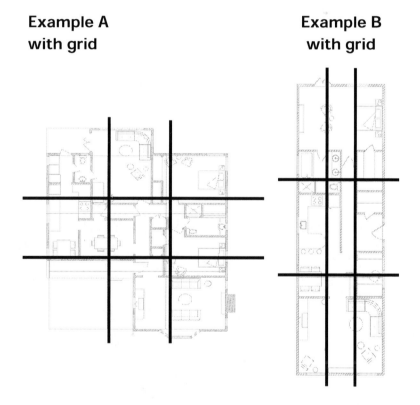

The Compass Reading

The next step is to determine the alignment of your house with the earth's magnetic fields by taking a compass reading. It is very important to take an accurate reading and not guess the orientation based on the direction of the sun or a map.

Why Do You Need To Use A Compass?

In Feng Shui, we look at the eight cardinal and inter-cardinal directions: East, Southeast, South, Southwest, West, Northwest, North, and Northeast when analyzing a home or building. Each of these directions holds unique significance to these buildings. If you do not use a compass to determine the correct orientation, you might completely misread your home. You cannot map the qi within the building without an exact orientation. It is similar to finding your way out of a forest without a compass. You have a high probability of getting lost. Without a compass, it simply is not Feng Shui.

A Compass vs. A Luopan

You can use any compass if you do not have a Luopan. The Luopan is simply a Chinese compass that helps determine the sitting direction of a building. It also contains a wealth of information on its dial that is used for more advanced applications. In recent years, Master Larry Sang simplified the traditional Luopan specifically for training Western students. Although it looks simple compared to an original Luopan, it has all the tools you need to accurately analyze a building. An important fact to remember about a Luopan is that it points to the South. The following information and instructions apply to a Luopan, however, if you are using a Western compass these concepts are easy to adapt.

Sang's Luopan

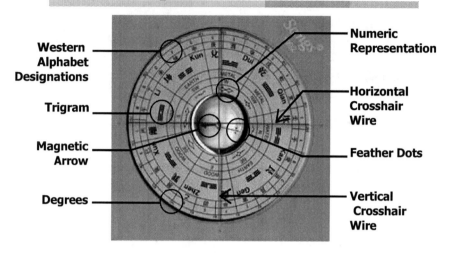

Western Alphabet Designations

Trigram

Magnetic Arrow

Degrees

Numeric Representation

Horizontal Crosshair Wire

Feather Dots

Vertical Crosshair Wire

Parts of Sang's Luopan

The Magnetic Arrow - The arrowhead points South rather than North. Western compasses point North.

The Feather Dots - (The twin dots at the center of the rotating dial). Always adjust the rotating (gold) dial to align the twin dots with the feather end of the arrow.

The Numeric Representations - The innermost ring has a dot pattern that represents the Trigrams' numbers. For example, Kun has two dots and Qian has six dots.

Crosshair Alignments - The red crosshairs designate the facing and sitting directions. Once the arrow is steady and the feather end is aligned over the north twin dots, you can determine the sitting direction and the facing direction.

The Eight Trigrams - The Eight Trigrams are the basis for orientation in Feng Shui and are shown on the Luopan with their respective elements, symbols, and directions.

Western Alphabet Designations - Each Trigram is divided into three equal parts. These parts are shown with both their Chinese symbols and using the Western Alphabet.

The Degrees - Outermost on the dial are the Western compass degrees in Arabic numerals.

General Guidelines for using the Luopan:

To use the Luopan or compass correctly, remember the following guidelines:

1. Always stand straight and upright.

2. Do not wear metal jewelry or belt buckles that can skew the compass.

3. Avoid any electrical influences such as automobiles or electrical boxes.

4. Always stand parallel to the building.

5. Keep your feet square below you.

6. You can keep the Luopan in the lower box case to manage it better.

Taking a reading with the Luopan:

With the general guidelines for using a luopan in mind, now you are ready to take a reading to determine which wall or corner of your home is located closest to North.

1. Take your reading outside, standing parallel to your home with your back to it. Stand straight and hold the Luopan at waist level. Wait until the arrow ceases to quiver.

2. Slowly turn the center (gold) dial so that the North/feather dots align with the feather of the arrow. If using a Western compass, turn the compass so that the needle's arrow end aligns with north (between 337.5 - 22.5 degrees).

3. Please take at least three separate readings from other positions. If you find that there is a discrepancy, take various readings at various locations until you are sure which one is correct. One direction should stand out as being correct.

4. Indicate on your floor plan which section is North. Fill in the other directions as illustrated. Please note that North can lie in a corner section.

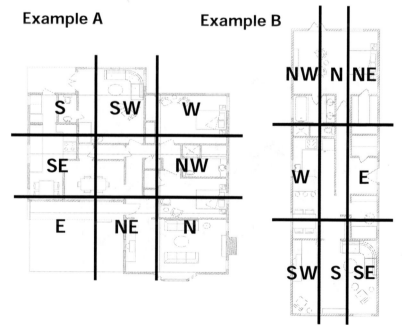

Example A   **Example B**

Directions to Avoid for Construction

The Three Sha and the Sui Po

* The **Three Sha** are in the **East**: **Yin**, **Mao**, and **Chen** directions.

* The **Sui Po** or **Year Breaker** is in the **Southwest**: **Wei** direction.

* The **Tai Sui** is in the **Northeast**: **Chou** direction.

> Therefore, avoid using these directions:
> **Chou, Yin, Mao, Chen, and Wei**

Directions to Avoid

15° Direction	Degrees	45° Direction	Sang's Luopan Alpha Designation
Chou		NE	c
Yin			e
Jia			f
Mao	22.5° - 127.5°	E	g
Yi			h
Chen		SE	i
Wei	202.5° - 217.5°	SW	o

What should we avoid in these directions?

* New construction sitting in these directions
  (except Chou Northeast).
* Major renovation to buildings sitting in these directions
  (except Chou Northeast).
* Major renovation to this section of the house, regardless of the
  sitting direction.
* Burial of the deceased in these directions.
* Digging or breaking of earth in these directions. If digging
  cannot be avoided in any of these areas, then place a metal wind
  chime outside between the house and the digging site.
* In addition, Oxen or Sheep born in the second, sixth,
  or twelfth month of the lunar calendar should avoid attending
  funerals or burials.

Feng Shui
2009

Qi Pattern for 2009

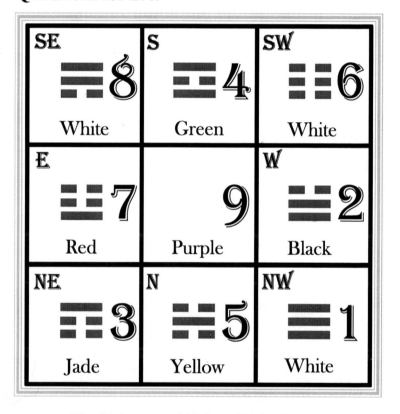

SE **8**	S **4**	SW **6**
White	Green	White
E **7**	**9**	W **2**
Red	Purple	Black
NE **3**	N **5**	NW **1**
Jade	Yellow	White

The Qi (energy) shift for 2009 begins on

February 4th, 2009 at 12:52 a.m.

Introduction

While this diagram may look foreign to the beginner, it is essential information for the experienced Feng Shui practitioner. Each year the qi pattern brings different effects. Some of these effects are quite auspicious and favorable and some may be inauspicious and not so favorable.

The effects of the 2009 energy pattern are analyzed for you in the following pages. Each analysis contains suggested remedies or enhancements for each section. Remedies are recommended to reduce negative qi. Enhancements are recommended to increase beneficial qi. These remedies or enhancements consist of the five elements: wood, fire, earth, metal, and water.

To use a remedy or enhancement, it must be placed inside the house within that particular section. If more than one room exists within a section, then each room needs to have its own remedy or enhancement. Any exceptions will be noted.

Feng Shui
2009

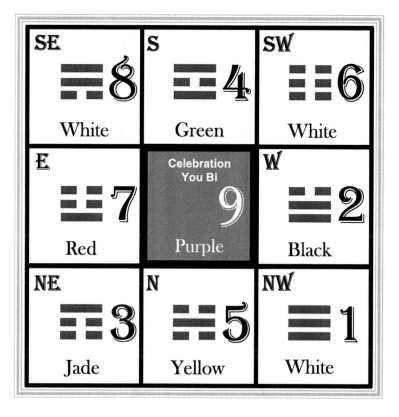

SE	S	SW
8 White	**4** Green	**6** White
E **7** Red	**Celebration You Bi** **9** Purple	**W** **2** Black
NE **3** Jade	**N** **5** Yellow	**NW** **1** White

The Center Section

Center

Analysis

Last year in this chapter, we predicted an elevated risk for earthquakes, landslides, floods, and water related disasters. 2009 will be quite similar to last year; it will not be a stable year.

In 2009, the *9 Purple You Bi Star* visits the center. This is a star that could be good or bad. It depends on how we make use of it. We are currently in Period 8, which is known as the **8 White Zuo Fu Star** and is earth element. As a result of the productive relationship between 9 Purple (fire) and 8 White (earth) in the center, we can predict that this year is beneficial for talented youthful leaders to take over the position of aging authorities.

However, Period 8 corresponds to Gen trigram in the *Yi Jing*. Gen represents the mountain. The 9 Purple Star represents Li trigram (Fire). Fire above Mountain forms hexagram 56, Lu. The meaning of this hexagram is "Traveling: On a journey, only minor undertakings go well." The image is a vivid one: Fire is spreading across a mountain. This is a dangerous sign for fire-related disasters such as earthquakes, forest fires, or terrorist bombings. Furthermore, people will experience global hyperinflation ahead. All the governments around the world can do very little about it. The Lu hexagram indicates "Only minor undertakings go well." However, the 9 Purple Star (fire element) is in a productive relationship with 8 White Zuo Fu Star (earth element), so 2009 will be turbulent but not totally bad. It will certainly not enter the territory of depression. Energy costs, home values, and wages all will reset back to their "real value." It is actually good in some ways.

Feng Shui

2009

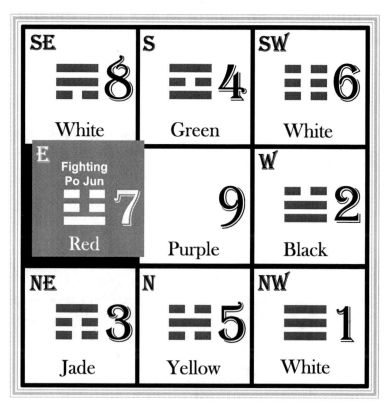

SE	S	SW
8 White	4 Green	6 White
E Fighting Po Jun 7 Red	9 Purple	**W** 2 Black
NE 3 Jade	N 5 Yellow	NW 1 White

The East Section

East

Situation

Doors, bedrooms, study rooms in the east section.

Analysis

The *7 Red Po Jun Star* visits the east in 2009. The 7 Red Star is metal element. It is a competitive and fighting star. It is also a star of breaking through, so it brings both promotion and fighting. The east section is the home of the **3 Jade Lu Cun Star**, which belongs to the wood element. The combination of the wood of 3 Jade and the metal of 7 Red create a domination relationship, since metal dominates wood. This makes the east section not so beneficial for break throughs in business and job or career switches. There is also the potential of leg injuries or throat discomfort if someone stays in this area more than eight hours per day.

Remedy

Use water element as a remedy in this sector. A fountain or aquarium in the east will help to change the poison into medicine.

After Remedy

Beneficial for business expansion and promotion, as well as for people who work in speech-related professions such as sales, singers, and fortune tellers.

Caution

If you use this section as an entrance, be on guard for break-ins.

Feng Shui
2009

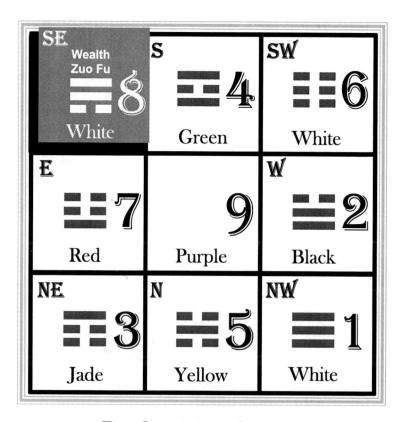

The Southeast Section

Southeast

Situation

Doors, bedrooms, study rooms in the southeast section.

Analysis

The *8 White Zuo Fu Wealth Star* visits the southeast in 2009. This 8 White Star brings wealth and fame. The element of the 8 White Star is earth. The southeast section is the home of the **4 Green Wen Qu Literary Star**, which is wood element. The combination of the wood of 4 Green and the earth of 8 White creates a domination relationship (wood dominates earth). This makes the southeast section not very beneficial for money luck, real estate development, or the construction business. There is also the potential of bone pain or broken limbs. Moreover, miscarriage easily arises in pregnant women, and it is also not beneficial for young people under 18 years of age. In 2009, the inauspicious Sui Sha Star is there, so avoid digging in the earth in this section to prevent some unhappy things from happening.

Remedy

Use fire element as a remedy in this sector. A fire remedy can be a red light bulb, a lamp with a red shade, or any red color item. The related colors of maroon, purple, or fuchsia may also be used.

After Remedy

Beneficial for money luck, pregnant women, teenagers, real estate, and the construction business.

Caution

Not beneficial for money luck, pregnant women, teenagers, real estate, and the construction business.

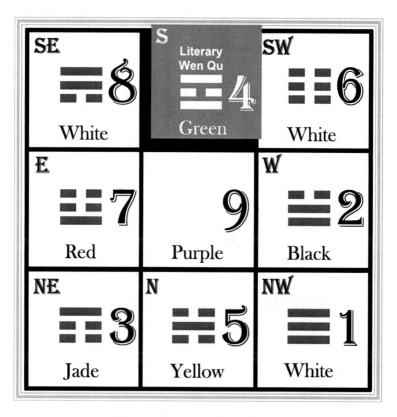

SE **8** White	S — Literary Wen Qu **4** Green	SW **6** White
E **7** Red	**9** Purple	W **2** Black
NE **3** Jade	N **5** Yellow	NW **1** White

The South Section

South

Situation

Doors, bedrooms, study rooms in the south section.

Analysis

This year the *4 Green Wen Qu Literary Star* falls in the south. This star also represents creative and academic achievement and Peach Blossom. The 4 Green Star's element is wood. The south is the home base of the *9 Purple Celebration Star*. It is fire element. Fire and wood create a harmonious relationship. Make use of this sector, as it will bring strong romantic qi (Peach Blossom) and good results in academia, for students, writers, and people working in the entertainment industry. It is especially beneficial for bringing in things to celebrate, such as a new life partner, marriage, job promotion, or receiving some kind of special honor.

Benefits

Prosperous for fire related business. Strong in Peach Blossom luck for females, bringing the opportunity to get married. Good results in academia, for students, writers, and people working in the entertainment industry.

Caution

Not beneficial for jewelers, goldsmiths, or metal related businesses. If this sector is the main entrance, housewives should be on guard as romantic affairs are easily aroused.

Feng Shui

2009

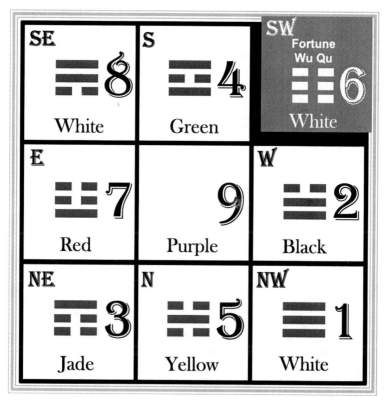

SE	S	SW
☷ **8** White	☳ **4** Green	**Fortune** **Wu Qu** ☶ **6** White
E ☵ **7** Red	**9** Purple	W ☱ **2** Black
NE ☵ **3** Jade	N ☴ **5** Yellow	NW ☰ **1** White

The Southwest Section

Southwest

Situation

Doors, bedrooms, study rooms in the southwest section.

Analysis

The *6 White Wu Qu Fortune Star* visits the southwest in 2009. The 6 White Star's element is metal. It is a star of authority and power and also brings wealth. The southwest section is the home of the *2 Black Ju Men Star*. The 2 Black Star is earth element. Earth and metal are in a productive relationship. Moreover, there are some additional yearly auspicious stars that fall into southwest sector making the southwest a beneficial section in the year of the Ox. Using this section will benefit politicians, the self-employed, salaried workers, and metal related businesses such as silver goods, jewelry, and goldsmiths. With hard work, substantial rewards can be expected. Southwest bedrooms are beneficial for finding a compatible life partner or having a baby.

Benefits

Beneficial for politicians, the self-employed, salaried workers and metal related businesses such as silver goods, jewelry, and goldsmiths.

Caution

If your main entrance is located here, do not use underhanded ways or take short cuts to make money. It may get you into trouble with the law. This is because the yearly inauspicious Guan Fu star is in southwest.

feng shui 風水

Feng Shui

2009

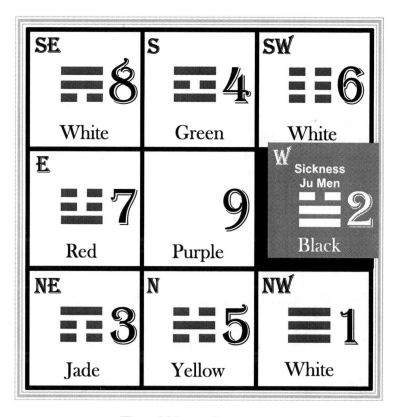

SE 8 White	**S** 4 Green	**SW** 6 White
E 7 Red	9 Purple	**W** Sickness Ju Men 2 Black
NE 3 Jade	**N** 5 Yellow	**NW** 1 White

The West Section

West

Situation

Doors, bedrooms, study rooms in the west section.

Analysis

The *2 Black Ju Men Star* visits the west this year. Its element is earth. It represents sickness, gossip and misunderstandings. The west is the home of the *7 Red Star*, which is metal element and has a fighting nature. Even though metal and earth are in a productive relationship and auspicious stars such as the Golden Cabinet, Tian Jie and Ba Zou also gather here, the west section is good and bad mixed. The potential for good fortune is there, but it is also easy to encounter fighting, gossip, legal problems and illness. Be on guard for these problems if you use this section as the main entrance. However, the productive relationship of metal and earth together with the auspicious Golden Cabinet Star make this sector strong in money luck. It will be quite beneficial for the self-employed to expand their business.

Benefits

Beneficial for hospitals, clinics, medicine, doctors, attorneys and businesses related to metal or entertainment.

Caution

Be on guard for fighting, gossip, legal problems and illness.

Feng Shui

2009

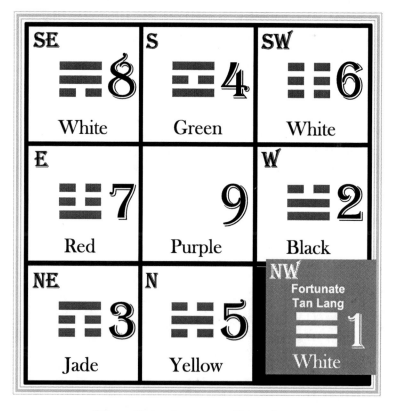

SE	S	SW
☳ 8	☵ 4	☷ 6
White	Green	White
E		W
☶ 7	9	☱ 2
Red	Purple	Black
NE	N	NW — Fortunate Tan Lang
☶ 3	☵ 5	☰ 1
Jade	Yellow	White

The Northwest Section

Northwest

Situation

Doors, bedrooms, study rooms in the northwest section.

Analysis

The *1 White Tan Lang Fortunate Star* is in the northwest this year. Its element is water. This Fortunate Star brings wealth, fame, romance, and benefit from negotiation. The northwest is the home of the *6 White Fortune Star*, which is metal element. The productive relationship of metal and water make this sector strong both in money luck and Peach Blossom. The 6 White (metal) provides energy to the 1 White (water) so it becomes a wealth-making and power-enhancing sector. However, auspicious yearly stars Yi Ma and Tian Yi mix with an inauspicious star of contention, Xing Chong, in the northwest. Under the influence of these annual stars, it is quite beneficial for venturing overseas. However, be careful of conflict with others that mostly arises due to challenges to the power of the authorities.

Benefits

Beneficial for bankers, loan officers, public relationships, and water related businesses or the entertainment industry, such as bars, nightclubs and casinos. Strong for Peach Blossom.

Caution

Conflicts, arguments and misunderstandings are easily aroused.

Feng Shui

2009

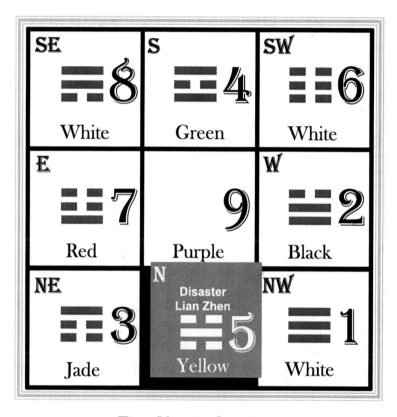

SE ☶ 8 White	**S** ☵ 4 Green	**SW** ☳ 6 White
E ☶ 7 Red	9 Purple	**W** ☱ 2 Black
NE ☵ 3 Jade	**N** Disaster Lian Zhen ☱ 5 Yellow	**NW** ☰ 1 White

The North Section

North

Situation

Doors, bedrooms, study rooms in the north section.

Analysis

The *5 Yellow Lian Zhen Disaster Star* is in the north this year. The 5 Yellow Star stands for delays, obstacles, fires, lawsuits, sickness, and casualties. Its element is earth. The north is the home of the **1 White Fortune Star**, and it is water element. The 1 White (water) and the 5 Yellow (earth) are in domination relationship. Additional inauspicious stars, Bing Fu and Gu Xu, also gather in the north, making it the most unfavorable section during the year of the Ox, 2009. If unfortunately the main entrance or bedroom falls in this sector and no remedy is applied, an unexpected casualty is quite possible. To prevent the occurrence of misfortune, it is inadvisable to dig in the earth or do construction inside or outside the house in the north.

Benefits

Encountering obstacles, pressure, delays, sickness, fighting, accidents, and unexpected casualties.

Caution

To reduce the potential negative effects, use the metal element as a remedy. A metal remedy can consist of metal décor, such as a piece of sculpture or an ornament. A metal remedy that has moving metal parts, such as grandfather clock, is most preferable.

Feng Shui
2009

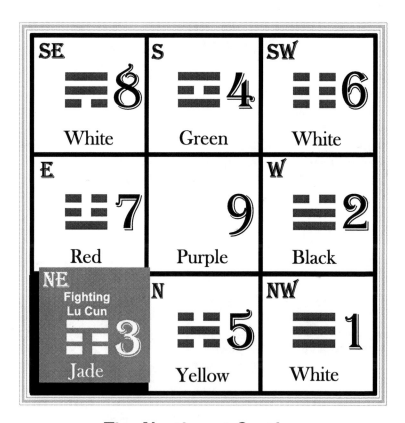

SE ☷ **8** White	**S** ☳ **4** Green	**SW** ☶ **6** White
E ☵ **7** Red	**9** Purple	**W** ☱ **2** Black
NE Fighting Lu Cun ☳ **3** Jade	**N** ☴ **5** Yellow	**NW** ☰ **1** White

The Northeast Section

Northeast

Situation

Doors, bedrooms, study rooms in the northeast section.

Analysis

The *3 Jade Lu Cun Star* falls in the northeast this year. The 3 Jade Star is wood element. It represents ambition, expansion, promotions, gossip, arguments, misunderstandings, and robberies. The northeast is the home of the **8 White Zuo Fu Money Star** which brings fame and wealth. Its element is earth. Earth and wood are in a domination relationship. The inauspicious yearly Jie Sha (Robbery) Star also falls in the northeast together with the Tai Sui. If the main entrance is in this sector, it is not advisable to do any kind of career expansion or try for a break through. Home owners should not be too aggressive and should act within the confines of their abilities and try not to over-estimate themselves. As for health, a bedroom in this section is not beneficial for young people or pregnant women. There is also the potential of bone pain or injury to the four limbs.

Caution

Not beneficial for money luck, business expansion, pregnant women, teenagers, real estate, and the construction business. Avoid digging in the earth in this section to prevent some unhappy things from occurring.

Remedy

Similar to southeast sector, use the fire element as a remedy here. A fire remedy can be a red light bulb, a lamp with a red shade, or any red color item. The related colors of maroon, purple, or fuchsia may also be used.

After Remedy

Beneficial for wealth, young people, pregnant women, and earth-related businesses.

feng shui

一萬年太久

只爭朝夕

毛澤東

Ten thousand years is too long,

we should seize only today.

Mao Ze Dong

Day Selection

Day Selection

Introduction to Day Selection

Day Selection has been used for a long time in China. Every year, almanacs would be published giving the best days for important activities, as well as days to avoid. It is thought that a positive outcome is more likely when an activity is begun on an auspicious day. In English, we talk about getting things off to a good start, but have no particular methodology to do this.

There are three aspects to selecting a good day: picking a day that is good for the activity, avoiding a day that is bad for the activity, and picking a day that is not bad for the person(s) involved. In the calendar pages that follow, each day will list two or three activities that are auspicious or inauspicious on that day. If you wanted to pick a date to get married, you would first look for days that were considered good for weddings. In addition, you need to check the birth information of the bride and groom. If the bride is a Rabbit and the groom is a Rat, then you also need to avoid any days that say Bad for Rat or Bad for Rabbit, even if they are good for weddings in general.

In addition, there are some days that are not good for any important activity. Usually this is because the energy of heaven and earth is too strong or inharmonious on those days.

Day Selection is used for the first day of an activity. It does not affect a continued activity. For example, you should begin construction on a day that is good for groundbreaking, but it is not a problem if the construction is continued through a day that is bad for groundbreaking. The construction need not be stopped.

On the next page are definitions of the various activities included in Master Sang's Day Selection Calendar.

Calender Terminology Key

Animals:
Generally a bad day for a person born in the year of the animal listed. Even if an activity is listed as beneficial for that day, it will usually not be beneficial for that animal.

Begin Mission:
Good for beginning a new position, mission, or assignment.

Burial:
Good for burial.

Business:
Good for trade or business.

Buy Property:
Good for purchasing real estate.

Contracts:
Good for signing or entering into a contract, pact, or agreement.

Don't Do Important things:
A bad day for most activities.

Fix House:
Good for repairing the inside or outside of the house. Also for installing major appliances, such as the stove or oven.

Funeral:
Good for funerals.

Ground Breaking:
Good for beginning construction or disturbing the earth.

Lawsuits:
Good for filing a lawsuit or going to court.

Moving:
Good for moving or changing residences.

Planting:
Good for gardening or planting.

Prayer:
Good for praying for blessings or happiness.

School:
Good for admissions into a new school.

Travel:
Good for going out or beginning a trip.

Wedding:
Good for marriage ceremonies or becoming engaged to be married.

Worship:
Good for rituals, rites, ceremonies, offering sacrifices, or honoring ancestors or the dead.

January

Sunday	Monday	Tuesday	Wednesday	Thursday	Friday	Saturday
				1 DON'T DO IMPORTANT THINGS — Bad for Rat	**2** Good for: Prayer, worship — Bad for Ox	**3** Good for: Grand opening, moving, wedding — Bad for Tiger
4 Bad for: Ground breaking, wedding — Bad for Rabbit	**5** Good for: Prayer, worship — Bad for Dragon	**6** Good for: School, worship — Bad for Snake	**7** Good for: School, begin mission — Bad for Horse	**8** Bad for: Lawsuit, wedding — Bad for Sheep	**9** Bad for: Fix house, travel — Bad for Monkey	**10** Good for: Lawsuit, wedding, ground breaking — Bad for Rooster
11 Bad for: Wedding, grand opening, ground breaking — Bad for Dog	**12** Bad for: Contract, wedding — Bad for Pig	**13** DON'T DO IMPORTANT THINGS — Bad for Rat	**14** DON'T DO IMPORTANT THINGS — Bad for Ox	**15** Good for: Begin mission, grand opening, ground breaking — Bad for Tiger	**16** Good for: Wedding, fix house, grand opening — Bad for Rabbit	**17** Good for: Planting, prayer — Bad for Dragon
18 Bad for: Business, lawsuit, wedding — Bad for Snake	**19** Good for: Burial, worship, ground breaking — Bad for Horse	**20** Good for: Prayer, worship — Bad for Sheep	**21** Bad for: Business, travel — Bad for Monkey	**22** Good for: Planting, prayer — Bad for Rooster	**23** Bad for: Ground breaking, wedding — Bad for Dog	**24** Good for: Contract, fix house, wedding — Bad for Pig
25 DON'T DO IMPORTANT THINGS — Bad for Rat	**26** DON'T DO IMPORTANT THINGS — Bad for Ox	**27** Bad for: Business, grand opening — Bad for Tiger	**28** Good for: Grand opening, moving, wedding — Bad for Rabbit	**29** Bad for: Business, contract — Bad for Dragon	**30** Good for: Grand opening, ground breaking, fix house — Bad for Snake	**31** Good for: Burial, worship — Bad for Horse

82

February 2009

Sunday	Monday	Tuesday	Wednesday	Thursday	Friday	Saturday
1 **Bad for:** Burial, grand opening, ground breaking Bad for Sheep	**2** **Bad for:** Wedding moving, travel Bad for Monkey	**3** DON'T DO IMPORTANT THINGS Bad for Rooster	**4** **Bad for:** Business, contract, lawsuit Bad for Dog	**5** DON'T DO IMPORTANT THINGS Bad for Pig	**6** **Good for:** Grand opening, wedding, business Bad for Rat	**7** DON'T DO IMPORTANT THINGS Bad for Ox
8 DON'T DO IMPORTANT THINGS Bad for Tiger	**9** **Good for:** Burial, prayer, worship Bad for Rabbit	**10** **Good for:** Fix house, ground breaking, enter school Bad for Dragon	**11** **Good for:** Grand opening, wedding, business Bad for Snake	**12** **Good for:** Enter school, contract, worship Bad for Horse	**13** **Bad for:** Wedding, grand opening, ground breaking Bad for Sheep	**14** **Good for:** Prayer, business Bad for Monkey
15 **Good for:** Ground breaking, moving, wedding Bad for Rooster	**16** **Good for:** Wedding, grand opening, ground breaking Bad for Dog	**17** DON'T DO IMPORTANT THINGS Bad for Pig	**18** **Good for:** Fix house, wedding, grand opening Bad for Rat	**19** DON'T DO IMPORTANT THINGS Bad for Ox	**20** DON'T DO IMPORTANT THINGS Bad for Tiger	**21** **Good for:** Moving, wedding, begin mission Bad for Rabbit
22 **Good for:** Prayer, worship Bad for Dragon	**23** **Good for:** Ground breaking, moving, wedding Bad for Snake	**24** **Good for:** Enter school, business, contract Bad for Horse	**25** DON'T DO IMPORTANT THINGS Bad for Sheep	**26** **Good for:** Business, contract, burial Bad for Monkey	**27** **Good for:** Worship, prayer, funeral Bad for Rooster	**28** **Good for:** Worship, prayer Bad for Dog

March 2009

Sunday	Monday	Tuesday	Wednesday	Thursday	Friday	Saturday
1 **Bad for:** Wedding, grand opening, fix house Bad for Pig	**2** **Good for:** Moving, wedding, grand opening Bad for Rat	**3** DON'T DO IMPORTANT THINGS Bad for Ox	**4** DON'T DO IMPORTANT THINGS Bad for Tiger	**5** DON'T DO IMPORTANT THINGS Bad for Rabbit	**6** **Bad for:** Business, contract, wedding Bad for Dragon	**7** **Good for:** Wedding, grand opening, ground breaking Bad for Snake
8 DON'T DO IMPORTANT THINGS Bad for Horse	**9** **Good for:** Begin mission, business, moving Bad for Sheep	**10** **Good for:** Contract, burial, ground breaking Bad for Monkey	**11** **Good for:** Contract, prayer, worship Bad for Rooster	**12** **Good for:** Fix house, moving, ground breaking Bad for Dog	**13** **Good for:** Contract, grand opening, buy property Bad for Pig	**14** **Good for:** Prayer, worship Bad for Rat
15 DON'T DO IMPORTANT THINGS Bad for Ox	**16** **Bad for:** Travel, wedding Bad for Tiger	**17** DON'T DO IMPORTANT THINGS Bad for Rabbit	**18** **Bad for:** Contract, lawsuit Bad for Dragon	**19** DON'T DO IMPORTANT THINGS Bad for Snake	**20** **Good for:** Prayer, worship Bad for Horse	**21** **Good for:** Grand opening, moving, wedding Bad for Sheep
22 **Good for:** Burial, planting, ground breaking Bad for Monkey	**23** **Good for:** Business, contract, fix house Bad for Rooster	**24** **Good for:** Worship, begin mission, enter school Bad for Dog	**25** **Good for:** Grand opening, prayer, worship Bad for Pig	**26** **Good for:** Prayer, worship Bad for Rat	**27** DON'T DO IMPORTANT THINGS Bad for Ox	**28** **Bad for:** Wedding, begin mission Bad for Tiger
29 DON'T DO IMPORTANT THINGS Bad for Rabbit	**30** **Good for:** Grand opening, moving, wedding Bad for Dragon	**31** **Good for:** Fix house, moving, ground breaking Bad for Snake				

April 2009

Sunday	Monday	Tuesday	Wednesday	Thursday	Friday	Saturday
			1 Bad for: Ground breaking, travel, wedding — Bad for Horse	**2** Good for: Grand opening, moving, wedding — Bad for Sheep	**3** Good for: Ground breaking, burial, planting — Bad for Monkey	**4** DON'T DO IMPORTANT THINGS — Bad for Rooster
5 DON'T DO IMPORTANT THINGS — Bad for Dog	**6** Bad for: Buy property, contract, wedding — Bad for Pig	**7** Good for: Grand opening, moving, wedding — Bad for Rat	**8** DON'T DO IMPORTANT THINGS — Bad for Ox	**9** Bad for: Begin mission, travel, wedding — Bad for Tiger	**10** Good for: Grand opening, business, wedding — Bad for Rabbit	**11** DON'T DO IMPORTANT THINGS — Bad for Dragon
12 Good for: Fix house, moving, ground breaking — Bad for Snake	**13** Good for: Wedding, grand opening, ground breaking — Bad for Horse	**14** Good for: Prayer, worship — Bad for Sheep	**15** Good for: Wedding, grand opening, begin mission — Bad for Monkey	**16** DON'T DO IMPORTANT THINGS — Bad for Rooster	**17** Good for: Prayer, worship — Bad for Dog	**18** Good for: Fix house, ground breaking, grand opening — Bad for Pig
19 Good for: Planting, prayer, worship — Bad for Rat	**20** DON'T DO IMPORTANT THINGS — Bad for Ox	**21** Good for: Burial, worship, ground breaking — Bad for Tiger	**22** Good for: Wedding, begin mission, grand opening — Bad for Rabbit	**23** DON'T DO IMPORTANT THINGS — Bad for Dragon	**24** Good for: Burial, planting — Bad for Snake	**25** Good for: Wedding, grand opening, ground breaking — Bad for Horse
26 Good for: Prayer, worship — Bad for Sheep	**27** Good for: Fix house, wedding, grand opening — Bad for Monkey	**28** Bad for: Moving, travel — Bad for Rooster	**29** Bad for: Begin mission, lawsuit, wedding — Bad for Dog	**30** DON'T DO IMPORTANT THINGS — Bad for Pig		

May 2009

Sunday	Monday	Tuesday	Wednesday	Thursday	Friday	Saturday
					1 Good for: Prayer, worship Bad for Rat	**2** DON'T DO IMPORTANT THINGS Bad for Ox
3 Bad for: Wedding, grand opening Bad for Tiger	**4** Good for: Moving, begin mission, grand opening Bad for Rabbit	**5** Good for: Wedding, grand opening, ground breaking Bad for Dragon	**6** DON'T DO IMPORTANT THINGS Bad for Snake	**7** DON'T DO IMPORTANT THINGS Bad for Horse	**8** Good for: Fix house, begin mission, ground breaking Bad for Sheep	**9** Bad for: Begin mission, lawsuit, travel Bad for Monkey
10 Good for: Wedding, grand opening, ground breaking Bad for Rooster	**11** Bad for: Grand opening, wedding, burial Bad for Dog	**12** Good for: Planting, begin mission, enter school Bad for Pig	**13** Good for: Worship Bad for Rat	**14** DON'T DO IMPORTANT THINGS Bad for Ox	**15** Good for: Grand opening, burial, moving Bad for Tiger	**16** Good for: Wedding, grand opening, ground breaking Bad for Rabbit
17 Good for: Wedding, grand opening, ground breaking Bad for Pig	**18** DON'T DO IMPORTANT THINGS Bad for Snake	**19** Bad for: Wedding, begin mission, grand opening Bad for Horse	**20** Good for: Grand opening, business, wedding Bad for Sheep	**21** Good for: Begin mission, moving, wedding Bad for Monkey	**22** Good for: Prayer, worship Bad for Rooster	**23** DON'T DO IMPORTANT THINGS Bad for Dog
24 Bad for: Business, travel Bad for Dragon	**25** Good for: Wedding, grand opening, ground breaking Bad for Rat	**26** DON'T DO IMPORTANT THINGS Bad for Ox	**27** Good for: Prayer, worship Bad for Tiger	**28** Good for: Wedding, grand opening, ground breaking Bad for Rabbit	**29** Good for: Prayer, worship Bad for Dragon	**30** DON'T DO IMPORTANT THINGS Bad for Snake
31 Good for: Begin mission, moving, travel Bad for Horse						

June 2009

Sunday	Monday	Tuesday	Wednesday	Thursday	Friday	Saturday
	1 Good for: Grand opening, fix house, wedding — Bad for Sheep	**2** Bad for: Lawsuit, begin mission — Bad for Monkey	**3** Good for: Prayer, worship, enter school — Bad for Rooster	**4** Good for: Prayer, worship — Bad for Dog	**5** Good for: Planting, prayer, worship — Bad for Pig	**6** Bad for: Wedding, begin mission — Bad for Rat
7 DON'T DO IMPORTANT THINGS — Bad for Ox	**8** Good for: Wedding, ground breaking, grand opening — Bad for Tiger	**9** Bad for: Ground breaking, fix house, travel — Bad for Rabbit	**10** Good for: Wedding, grand opening, ground breaking — Bad for Dragon	**11** Good for: Worship — Bad for Snake	**12** DON'T DO IMPORTANT THINGS — Bad for Horse	**13** Good for: Worship, prayer — Bad for Sheep
14 Good for: Business, wedding grand opening — Bad for Monkey	**15** Good for: Worship — Bad for Rooster	**16** Good for: Moving, begin mission, ground breaking — Bad for Dog	**17** Bad for: Travel, moving — Bad for Pig	**18** Good for: Prayer, worship — Bad for Rat	**19** DON'T DO IMPORTANT THINGS — Bad for Ox	**20** DON'T DO IMPORTANT THINGS — Bad for Tiger
21 Bad for: Business, moving, buy property — Bad for Rabbit	**22** Good for: Planting, prayer, worship — Bad for Dragon	**23** Good for: Worship — Bad for Snake	**24** DON'T DO IMPORTANT THINGS — Bad for Horse	**25** Good for: Worship, prayer — Bad for Sheep	**26** Good for: Wedding, grand opening, ground breaking — Bad for Monkey	**27** Good for: Worship — Bad for Rooster
28 Good for: Prayer, worship — Bad for Dog	**29** DON'T DO IMPORTANT THINGS — Bad for Pig	**30** Bad for: Wedding, grand opening — Bad for Rat				

July 2009

Sunday	Monday	Tuesday	Wednesday	Thursday	Friday	Saturday
			1 DON'T DO IMPORTANT THINGS — Bad for Ox	**2** Good for: Wedding, grand opening, ground breaking — Bad for Tiger	**3** Good for: Prayer, worship — Bad for Rabbit	**4** Good for: Wedding, burial, ground breaking — Bad for Dragon
5 Good for: Worship — Bad for Snake	**6** DON'T DO IMPORTANT THINGS — Bad for Horse	**7** DON'T DO IMPORTANT THINGS — Bad for Sheep	**8** Good for: Business, contract, ground breaking — Bad for Monkey	**9** Good for: Grand opening, moving, wedding — Bad for Rooster	**10** Good for: Business, planting, worship — Bad for Dog	**11** Bad for: Wedding, grand opening, ground breaking — Bad for Pig
12 Good for: Worship — Bad for Rat	**13** DON'T DO IMPORTANT THINGS — Bad for Ox	**14** Good for: Prayer, worship — Bad for Tiger	**15** Good for: Worship — Bad for Rabbit	**16** Bad for: Wedding, grand opening, ground breaking — Bad for Dragon	**17** Bad for: Wedding, burial, ground breaking — Bad for Snake	**18** Good for: Wedding, fix house, ground breaking — Bad for Horse
19 DON'T DO IMPORTANT THINGS — Bad for Sheep	**20** Good for: Begin mission, fix house, grand opening — Bad for Monkey	**21** Good for: Grand opening, moving, wedding — Bad for Rooster	**22** Good for: Worship — Bad for Dog	**23** Good for: Worship, begin mission, enter school — Bad for Pig	**24** Good for: Worship, burial, ground breaking — Bad for Rat	**25** DON'T DO IMPORTANT THINGS — Bad for Ox
26 Good for: Worship — Bad for Tiger	**27** Good for: Prayer, worship — Bad for Rabbit	**28** Good for: Prayer, worship — Bad for Dragon	**29** Good for: Moving, begin mission, ground breaking — Bad for Snake	**30** DON'T DO IMPORTANT THINGS — Bad for Horse	**31** DON'T DO IMPORTANT THINGS — Bad for Sheep	

August 2009

Sunday	Monday	Tuesday	Wednesday	Thursday	Friday	Saturday
						1 — Good for: Moving, grand opening, ground breaking — Bad for Monkey
2 — Good for: Grand opening, fix house, wedding — Bad for Rooster	**3** — Bad for: Grand opening, business, lawsuit — Bad for Dog	**4** — Good for: Worship, begin mission, enter school — Bad for Pig	**5** — Good for: Ground breaking, burial, worship — Bad for Rat	**6** — DON'T DO IMPORTANT THINGS — Bad for Ox	**7** — Good for: Begin mission, wedding, worship — Bad for Tiger	**8** — Good for: Burial, ground breaking — Bad for Rabbit
9 — Good for: Planting, prayer, worship — Bad for Dragon	**10** — Good for: Begin mission, business, moving — Bad for Snake	**11** — Good for: Wedding, grand opening, ground breaking — Bad for Horse	**12** — Good for: Planting, worship — Bad for Sheep	**13** — DON'T DO IMPORTANT THINGS — Bad for Monkey	**14** — Good for: Worship — Bad for Rooster	**15** — Good for: Fix house, grand opening, ground breaking — Bad for Dog
16 — Good for: Wedding, grand opening, ground breaking — Bad for Pig	**17** — Good for: Worship, enter school, begin mission — Bad for Rat	**18** — DON'T DO IMPORTANT THINGS — Bad for Ox	**19** — Good for: Prayer, worship — Bad for Tiger	**20** — Good for: Ground breaking, burial, fix house — Bad for Rabbit	**21** — Good for: Wedding, grand opening, ground breaking — Bad for Dragon	**22** — Good for: Prayer, worship — Bad for Snake
23 — Good for: Wedding, begin mission, grand opening — Bad for Horse	**24** — Bad for: Wedding, grand opening, begin mission — Bad for Sheep	**25** — DON'T DO IMPORTANT THINGS — Bad for Monkey	**26** — Good for: Wedding, burial, moving — Bad for Rooster	**27** — Good for: Prayer, worship — Bad for Dog	**28** — Bad for: Business, grand opening — Bad for Pig	**29** — Good for: Worship, enter school — Bad for Rat
30 — DON'T DO IMPORTANT THINGS — Bad for Ox	**31** — Good for: Begin mission, burial, wedding — Bad for Tiger					

September 2009

Sunday	Monday	Tuesday	Wednesday	Thursday	Friday	Saturday
		1 Good for: Burial, ground breaking — Bad for Rabbit	**2** Good for: Planting, prayer, worship — Bad for Dragon	**3** Good for: Prayer, worship — Bad for Snake	**4** Good for: Grand opening, moving, wedding — Bad for Horse	**5** Good for: Burial, worship, ground breaking — Bad for Sheep
6 DON'T DO IMPORTANT THINGS — Bad for Monkey	**7** DON'T DO IMPORTANT THINGS — Bad for Rooster	**8** Bad for: Lawsuit, wedding — Bad for Dog	**9** Good for: Grand opening, moving, wedding — Bad for Pig	**10** Good for: Prayer, worship — Bad for Rat	**11** DON'T DO IMPORTANT THINGS — Bad for Ox	**12** Good for: Contract, burial, ground breaking — Bad for Tiger
13 Good for: Planting, prayer, worship — Bad for Rabbit	**14** Good for: Contract, begin mission, buy property — Bad for Dragon	**15** Bad for: Wedding, grand opening, ground breaking — Bad for Snake	**16** Bad for: Business, contract, wedding — Bad for Horse	**17** Good for: Wedding, grand opening, ground breaking — Bad for Sheep	**18** Bad for: Ground breaking, burial, wedding — Bad for Monkey	**19** DON'T DO IMPORTANT THINGS — Bad for Rooster
20 Bad for: Wedding, grand opening, ground breaking — Bad for Dog	**21** Good for: Wedding, burial, moving — Bad for Pig	**22** DON'T DO IMPORTANT THINGS — Bad for Rat	**23** DON'T DO IMPORTANT THINGS — Bad for Ox	**24** Bad for: Business, buy property, grand opening — Bad for Tiger	**25** Good for: Prayer, worship — Bad for Rabbit	**26** Good for: Begin mission, business, worship — Bad for Dragon
27 Good for: Contract, moving, wedding — Bad for Snake	**28** Good for: Worship — Bad for Horse	**29** Good for: Wedding, ground breaking — Bad for Sheep	**30** Bad for: Ground breaking, wedding, burial — Bad for Monkey			

October 2009

Sunday	Monday	Tuesday	Wednesday	Thursday	Friday	Saturday
				1 DON'T DO IMPORTANT THINGS — Bad for Rooster	**2** Good for: Wedding, grand opening, ground breaking — Bad for Dog	**3** Good for: Ground breaking business, wedding — Bad for Pig
4 Good for: Prayer, worship — Bad for Rat	**5** DON'T DO IMPORTANT THINGS — Bad for Ox	**6** Good for: Burial, planting, ground breaking — Bad for Tiger	**7** Good for: Prayer, worship — Bad for Rabbit	**8** Good for: Burial, moving, wedding — Bad for Dragon	**9** DON'T DO IMPORTANT THINGS — Bad for Snake	**10** Good for: Worship — Bad for Horse
11 Bad for: Grand opening, wedding, burial — Bad for Sheep	**12** Bad for: Burial, funeral, lawsuit — Bad for Monkey	**13** Good for: Wedding, grand opening, ground breaking — Bad for Rooster	**14** DON'T DO IMPORTANT THINGS — Bad for Dog	**15** Good for: Ground breaking, moving, wedding — Bad for Pig	**16** Good for: Grand opening, fix house, wedding — Bad for Rat	**17** DON'T DO IMPORTANT THINGS — Bad for Ox
18 Good for: Wedding, begin mission, ground breaking — Bad for Tiger	**19** Bad for: Wedding, grand opening, ground breaking — Bad for Rabbit	**20** DON'T DO IMPORTANT THINGS — Bad for Dragon	**21** Bad for: Burial, ground breaking, grand opening — Bad for Snake	**22** Good for: Worship — Bad for Horse	**23** Good for: Prayer, worship — Bad for Sheep	**24** Bad for: Wedding, begin mission, grand opening — Bad for Monkey
25 Good for: Ground breaking, contract, wedding — Bad for Rooster	**26** DON'T DO IMPORTANT THINGS — Bad for Dog	**27** Good for: Planting, prayer, worship — Bad for Pig	**28** Good for: Wedding, grand opening, ground breaking — Bad for Rat	**29** DON'T DO IMPORTANT THINGS — Bad for Ox	**30** Good for: Fix house, moving, wedding — Bad for Tiger	**31** Bad for: Travel, ground breaking — Bad for Rabbit

November

2009

Sunday	Monday	Tuesday	Wednesday	Thursday	Friday	Saturday
1 Good for: Begin mission, moving, worship — Bad for Dragon	**2** Good for: Moving, prayer, worship — Bad for Snake	**3** Good for: Worship — Bad for Horse	**4** DON'T DO IMPORTANT THINGS — Bad for Sheep	**5** Bad for: Contract, wedding — Bad for Monkey	**6** DON'T DO IMPORTANT THINGS — Bad for Rooster	**7** Bad for: Business, contract, moving — Bad for Dog
8 DON'T DO IMPORTANT THINGS — Bad for Pig	**9** Good for: Worship — Bad for Rat	**10** DON'T DO IMPORTANT THINGS — Bad for Ox	**11** Good for: Ground breaking, fix house, moving — Bad for Tiger	**12** Good for: Enter school, begin mission — Bad for Rabbit	**13** Bad for: Funeral, wedding — Bad for Dragon	**14** DON'T DO IMPORTANT THINGS — Bad for Snake
15 Good for: Ground breaking, burial, wedding — Bad for Horse	**16** Good for: Worship — Bad for Sheep	**17** Good for: Wedding, grand opening, ground breaking — Bad for Monkey	**18** Good for: Grand opening, contract, wedding — Bad for Rooster	**19** Bad for: Business, lawsuit, grand opening — Bad for Dog	**20** DON'T DO IMPORTANT THINGS — Bad for Pig	**21** Good for: Wedding, begin mission, ground breaking — Bad for Rat
22 DON'T DO IMPORTANT THINGS — Bad for Ox	**23** Bad for: Funeral, wedding — Bad for Tiger	**24** Good for: Worship, enter school — Bad for Rabbit	**25** Good for: Prayer, worship — Bad for Dragon	**26** Good for: Planting, prayer, worship — Bad for Snake	**27** Good for: Moving, burial, ground breaking — Bad for Horse	**28** Good for: Worship — Bad for Sheep
29 Good for: Grand opening, moving, wedding — Bad for Monkey	**30** Good for: Wedding, grand opening, ground breaking — Bad for Rooster					

December 2009

Sunday	Monday	Tuesday	Wednesday	Thursday	Friday	Saturday
		1 Good for: Begin mission, business, wedding — Bad for Dog	**2** DON'T DO IMPORTANT THINGS — Bad for Pig	**3** Good for: Worship — Bad for Rat	**4** DON'T DO IMPORTANT THINGS — Bad for Ox	**5** Good for: Wedding, grand opening, ground breaking — Bad for Tiger
6 Good for: Ground breaking, burial, wedding — Bad for Rabbit	**7** Good for: Ground breaking, planting, fix house — Bad for Dragon	**8** Good for: Planting, worship — Bad for Snake	**9** Bad for: Wedding, begin mission — Bad for Horse	**10** Good for: Prayer, worship — Bad for Sheep	**11** Good for: Grand opening, wedding, business — Bad for Monkey	**12** DON'T DO IMPORTANT THINGS — Bad for Rooster
13 Good for: Fix house, contract, wedding — Bad for Dog	**14** Good for: Worship, burial, ground breaking — Bad for Pig	**15** DON'T DO IMPORTANT THINGS — Bad for Rat	**16** DON'T DO IMPORTANT THINGS — Bad for Ox	**17** Good for: Prayer, worship — Bad for Tiger	**18** Good for: Worship — Bad for Rabbit	**19** Bad for: Lawsuit, funeral — Bad for Dragon
20 Bad for: Moving, travel — Bad for Snake	**21** DON'T DO IMPORTANT THINGS — Bad for Horse	**22** Good for: Ground breaking, business, wedding — Bad for Sheep	**23** Good for: Fix house, wedding, contract — Bad for Monkey	**24** Bad for: Lawsuit, funeral — Bad for Rooster	**25** Good for: Wedding, begin mission, ground breaking — Bad for Dog	**26** Good for: Burial, worship, ground breaking — Bad for Pig
27 DON'T DO IMPORTANT THINGS — Bad for Rat	**28** DON'T DO IMPORTANT THINGS — Bad for Ox	**29** Good for: Grand opening, contract, wedding — Bad for Tiger	**30** DON'T DO IMPORTANT THINGS — Bad for Rabbit	**31** Good for: Ground breaking, worship, fix house — Bad for Dragon		

Sunday	Monday	Tuesday	Wednesday	Thursday	Friday	Saturday
					1 DON'T DO IMPORTANT THINGS — Bad for Snake	**2** **Bad for:** Wedding, grand opening, ground breaking — Bad for Horse
3 **Good for:** Grand opening, moving, wedding — Bad for Sheep	**4** **Good for:** Ground breaking, grand opening, begin mission — Bad for Monkey	**5** **Good for:** Grand opening, moving, wedding — Bad for Rooster	**6** **Bad for:** Burial, wedding, grand opening — Bad for Dog	**7** DON'T DO IMPORTANT THINGS — Bad for Pig	**8** **Bad for:** Grand opening, business, wedding — Bad for Rat	**9** DON'T DO IMPORTANT THINGS — Bad for Ox
10 **Good for:** Business, contract, grand opening — Bad for Tiger	**11** **Good for:** Grand opening, moving, wedding — Bad for Rabbit	**12** **Good for:** Prayer, worship — Bad for Dragon	**13** **Bad for:** Grand opening, business, wedding — Bad for Snake	**14** **Good for:** Ground breaking, burial, worship — Bad for Horse	**15** **Good for:** Prayer, worship — Bad for Sheep	**16** **Bad for:** Travel, moving, grand opening — Bad for Monkey
17 **Good for:** Prayer, worship — Bad for Rooster	**18** DON'T DO IMPORTANT THINGS — Bad for Dog	**19** **Good for:** Ground breaking, fix house, wedding — Bad for Pig	**20** **Good for:** Grand opening, moving, wedding — Bad for Rat	**21** DON'T DO IMPORTANT THINGS — Bad for Ox	**22** **Bad for:** Business, buy property, grand opening — Bad for Tiger	**23** **Good for:** Grand opening, contract, wedding — Bad for Rabbit
24 **Good for:** Prayer, worship — Bad for Dragon	**25** **Good for:** Enter school, grand opening, ground breaking — Bad for Snake	**26** **Good for:** Prayer, worship — Bad for Horse	**27** DON'T DO IMPORTANT THINGS — Bad for Sheep	**28** **Bad for:** Business, wedding — Bad for Monkey	**29** **Good for:** Grand opening, business, wedding — Bad for Rooster	**30** **Good for:** Prayer, worship — Bad for Dog
31 **Good for:** Ground breaking, business, moving — Bad for Pig						

Ten Thousand Year Calendar

2009

Ten-Thousand Year

YEAR: 2009	Ji Chou	9 Purple			
1ST MONTH Bing Yin	**2ND MONTH** Ding Mao	**3RD MONTH** Wu Chen	**4TH MONTH** Ji Si	**5TH MONTH** Geng Wu	**LEAP MONTH**
1 1/26 Xin Wei	2/25 Xin Chou	3/27 Xin Wei	4/25 Geng Zi	5/24 Ji Si	6/23 Ji Hai 1
2 1/27 Ren Shen	2/26 Ren Yin	3/28 Ren Shen	4/26 Xin Chou	5/25 Geng Wu	6/24 Geng Zi 2
3 1/28 Gui You	2/27 Gui Mao	3/29 Gui You	4/27 Ren Yin	5/26 Xin Wei	6/25 Xin Chou 3
4 1/29 Jia Xu	2/28 Jia Chen	3/30 Jia Xu	4/28 Gui Mao	5/27 Ren Shen	6/26 Ren Yin 4
5 1/30 Yi Hai	3/1 Yi Si	3/31 Yi Hai	4/29 Jia Chen	5/28 Gui You	6/27 Gui Mao 5
6 1/31 Bing Zi	3/2 Bing Wu	4/1 Bing Zi	4/30 Yi Si	5/29 Jia Xu	6/28 Jia Chen 6
7 2/1 Ding Chou	3/3 Ding Wei	4/2 Ding Chou	5/1 Bing Wu	5/30 Yi Hai	6/29 Yi Si 7
8 2/2 Wu Yin	3/4 Wu Shen	4/3 Wu Yin	5/2 Ding Wei	5/31 Bing Zi	6/30 Bing Wu 8
9 2/3 Ji Mao	3/5 Ji You	4/4 Ji Mao	5/3 Wu Shen	6/1 Ding Chou	7/1 Ding Wei 9
10 2/4 Geng Chen	3/6 Geng Xu	4/5 Geng Chen	5/4 Ji You	6/2 Wu Yin	7/2 Wu Shen 10
11 2/5 Xin Si	3/7 Xin Hai	4/6 Xin Si	5/5 Geng Xu	6/3 Ji Mao	7/3 Ji You 11
12 2/6 Ren Wu	3/8 Ren Zi	4/7 Ren Wu	5/6 Xin Hai	6/4 Geng Chen	7/4 Geng Xu 12
13 2/7 Gui Wei	3/9 Gui Chou	4/8 Gui Wei	5/7 Ren Zi	6/5 Xin Si	7/5 Xin Hai 13
14 2/8 Jia Shen	3/10 Jia Yin	4/9 Jia Shen	5/8 Gui Chou	6/6 Ren Wu	7/6 Ren Zi 14
15 2/9 Yi You	3/11 Yi Mao	4/10 Yi You	5/9 Jia Yin	6/7 Gui Wei	7/7 Gui Chou 15
16 2/10 Bing Xu	3/12 Bing Chen	4/11 Bing Xu	5/10 Yi Mao	6/8 Jia Shen	7/8 Jia Yin 16
17 2/11 Ding Hai	3/13 Ding Si	4/12 Ding Hai	5/11 Bing Chen	6/9 Yi You	7/9 Yi Mao 17
18 2/12 Wu Zi	3/14 Wu Wu	4/13 Wu Zi	5/12 Ding Si	6/10 Bing Xu	7/10 Bing Chen 18
19 2/13 Ji Chou	3/15 Ji Wei	4/14 Ji Chou	5/13 Wu Wu	6/11 Ding Hai	7/11 Ding Si 19
20 2/14 Geng Yin	3/16 Geng Shen	4/15 Geng Yin	5/14 Ji Wei	6/12 Wu Zi	7/12 Wu Wu 20
21 2/15 Xin Mao	3/17 Xin You	4/16 Xin Mao	5/15 Geng Shen	6/13 Ji Chou	7/13 Ji Wei 21
22 2/16 Ren Chen	3/18 Ren Xu	4/17 Ren Chen	5/16 Xin You	6/14 Geng Yin	7/14 Geng Shen 22
23 2/17 Gui Si	3/19 Gui Hai	4/18 Gui Si	5/17 Ren Xu	6/15 Xin Mao	7/15 Xin You 23
24 2/18 Jia Wu	3/20 Jia Zi	4/19 Jia Wu	5/18 Gui Hai	6/16 Ren Chen	7/16 Ren Xu 24
25 2/19 Yi Wei	3/21 Yi Chou	4/20 Yi Wei	5/19 Jia Zi	6/17 Gui Si	7/17 Gui Hai 25
26 2/20 Bing Shen	3/22 Bing Yin	4/21 Bing Shen	5/20 Yi Chou	6/18 Jia Wu	7/18 Jia Zi 26
27 2/21 Ding You	3/23 Ding Mao	4/22 Ding You	5/21 Bing Yin	6/19 Yi Wei	7/19 Yi Chou 27
28 2/22 Wu Xu	3/24 Wu Chen	4/23 Wu Xu	5/22 Ding Mao	6/20 Bing Shen	7/20 Bing Yin 28
29 2/23 Ji Hai	3/25 Ji Si	4/24 Ji Hai	5/23 Wu Chen	6/21 Ding You	7/21 Ding Mao 29
30 2/24 Geng Zi	3/26 Geng Wu			6/22 Wu Xu	30
	5 Yellow	4 Green	3 Jade	2 Black	1 White	
Jie	Li Chun 2/4 12:52a	Jing Zhi 3/5 7:02p	Qing Ming 4/5 12:05a	Li Xia 5/5 5:39p	Mang Zhong 6/5 10:01p	Jie
Qi	Yu Shui 2/18 8:46p	Chun Fen 3/20 7:59p	Gu Yu 4/20 7:18a	Xiao Man 5/21 6:40a	Xia Zhi 6/21 2:46p	Qi

Calendar

2009

	6TH MONTH Xin Wei	7TH MONTH Ren Shen	8TH MONTH Gui You	9TH MONTH Jia Xu	10TH MONTH Yi Hai	11TH MONTH Bing Zi	12TH MONTH Ding Chou	
						2009 - 2010		
1	7/22 Wu Chen	8/20 Ding You	9/19 Ding Mao	10/18 Bing Shen	11/17 Bing Yin	12/16 Yi Wei	1/15 Yi Chou	1
2	7/23 Ji Si	8/21 Wu Xu	9/20 Wu Chen	10/19 Ding You	11/18 Ding Mao	12/17 Bing Shen	1/16 Bing Yin	2
3	7/24 Geng Wu	8/22 Ji Hai	9/21 Ji Si	10/20 Wu Xu	11/19 Wu Chen	12/18 Ding You	1/17 Ding Mao	3
4	7/25 Xin Wei	8/23 Geng Zi	9/22 Geng Wu	10/21 Ji Hai	11/20 Ji Si	12/19 Wu Xu	1/18 Wu Chen	4
5	7/26 Ren Shen	8/24 Xin Chou	9/23 Xin Wei	10/22 Geng Zi	11/21 Geng Wu	12/20 Ji Hai	1/19 Ji Si	5
6	7/27 Gui You	8/25 Ren Yin	9/24 Ren Shen	10/23 Xin Chou	11/22 Xin Wei	12/21 Geng Zi	1/20 Geng Wu	6
7	7/28 Jia Xu	8/26 Gui Mao	9/25 Gui You	10/24 Ren Yin	11/23 Ren Shen	12/22 Xin Chou	1/21 Xin Wei	7
8	7/29 Yi Hai	8/27 Jia Chen	9/26 Jia Xu	10/25 Gui Mao	11/24 Gui You	12/23 Ren Yin	1/22 Ren Shen	8
9	7/30 Bing Zi	8/28 Yi Si	9/27 Yi Hai	10/26 Jia Chen	11/25 Jia Xu	12/24 Gui Mao	1/23 Gui You	9
10	7/31 Ding Chou	8/29 Bing Wu	9/28 Bing Zi	10/27 Yi Si	11/26 Yi Hai	12/25 Jia Chen	1/24 Jia Xu	10
11	8/1 Wu Yin	8/30 Ding Wei	9/29 Ding Chou	10/28 Bing Wu	11/27 Bing Zi	12/26 Yi Si	1/25 Yi Hai	11
12	8/2 Ji Mao	8/31 Wu Shen	9/30 Wu Yin	10/29 Ding Wei	11/28 Ding Chou	12/27 Bing Wu	1/26 Bing Zi	12
13	8/3 Geng Chen	9/1 Ji You	10/1 Ji Mao	10/30 Wu Shen	11/29 Wu Yin	12/28 Ding Wei	1/27 Ding Chou	13
14	8/4 Xin Si	9/2 Geng Xu	10/2 Geng Chen	10/31 Ji You	11/30 Ji Mao	12/29 Wu Shen	1/28 Wu Yin	14
15	8/5 Ren Wu	9/3 Xin Hai	10/3 Xin Si	11/1 Geng Xu	12/1 Geng Chen	12/30 Ji You	1/29 Ji Mao	15
16	8/6 Gui Wei	9/4 Ren Zi	10/4 Ren Wu	11/2 Xin Hai	12/2 Xin Si	12/31 Geng Xu	1/30 Geng Chen	16
17	8/7 Jia Shen	9/5 Gui Chou	10/5 Gui Wei	11/3 Ren Zi	12/3 Ren Wu	1/1 Xin Hai	1/31 Xin Si	17
18	8/8 Yi You	9/6 Jia Yin	10/6 Jia Shen	11/4 Gui Chou	12/4 Gui Wei	1/2 Ren Zi	2/1 Ren Wu	18
19	8/9 Bing Xu	9/7 Yi Mao	10/7 Yi You	11/5 Jia Yin	12/5 Jia Shen	1/3 Gui Chou	2/2 Gui Wei	19
20	8/10 Ding Hai	9/8 Bing Chen	10/8 Bing Xu	11/6 Yi Mao	12/6 Yi You	1/4 Jia Yin	2/3 Jia Shen	20
21	8/11 Wu Zi	9/9 Ding Si	10/9 Ding Hai	11/7 Bing Chen	12/7 Bing Xu	1/5 Yi Mao	2/4 Yi You	21
22	8/12 Ji Chou	9/10 Wu Wu	10/10 Wu Zi	11/8 Ding Si	12/8 Ding Hai	1/6 Bing Chen	2/5 Bing Xu	22
23	8/13 Geng Yin	9/11 Ji Wei	10/11 Ji Chou	11/9 Wu Wu	12/9 Wu Zi	1/7 Ding Si	2/6 Ding Hai	23
24	8/14 Xin Mao	9/12 Geng Shen	10/12 Geng Yin	11/10 Ji Wei	12/10 Ji Chou	1/8 Wu Wu	2/7 Wu Zi	24
25	8/15 Ren Chen	9/13 Xin You	10/13 Xin Mao	11/11 Geng Shen	12/11 Geng Yin	1/9 Ji Wei	2/8 Ji Chou	25
26	8/16 Gui Si	9/14 Ren Xu	10/14 Ren Chen	11/12 Xin You	12/12 Xin Mao	1/10 Geng Shen	2/9 Geng Yin	26
27	8/17 Jia Wu	9/15 Gui Hai	10/15 Gui Si	11/13 Ren Xu	12/13 Ren Chen	1/11 Xin You	2/10 Xin Mao	27
28	8/18 Yi Wei	9/16 Jia Zi	10/16 Jia Wu	11/14 Gui Hai	12/14 Gui Si	1/12 Ren Xu	2/11 Ren Chen	28
29	8/19 Bing Shen	9/17 Yi Chou	10/17 Yi Wei	11/15 Jia Zi	12/15 Jia Wu	1/13 Gui Hai	2/12 Gui Si	29
30		9/18 Bing Yin		11/16 Yi Chou		1/14 Jia Zi	2/13 Jia Wu	30
	9 Purple	8 White	7 Red	6 White	5 Yellow	4 Green	3 Jade	
Jie	Xiao Shu 7/7 8:24a	Li Qiu 8/7 6:07p	Bai Lu 9/7 8:51p	Han Lu 10/8 12:15p	Li Dong 11/7 3:10p	Da Xue 12/7 7:05a	Xiao Han 1/5 7:00p	Jie
Qi	Da Shu 7/23 1:39a	Chu Shu 8/23 8:35a	Qiu Fen 9/23 5:59a	Shuang Jiang 10/23 3:05p	Xiao Xue 11/22 12:27p	Dong Zhi 12/22 1:40a	Da Han 1/20 12:18p	Qi

AFSI Book Store

The Principles of Feng Shui -Book One

After years of intensive research, experimentation, exploration and teaching of Feng Shui, Master Larry Sang put forth his accumulated knowledge and insights into this book. This book will systematically introduce Feng Shui to its readers. This book is recommended for our Beginning, Intermediate and Advanced Feng Shui classes. Available in both paperback and ebook. $18.75 US

Sang's Luopan

The Luopan is a Chinese compass used in Feng Shui readings. It offers more information for a Feng Shui reading besides the cardinal and inter-cardinal directions. Whereas a Western compass may be used in Feng Shui, a Luopan saves several steps in calculations. The Luopan is 4 inches (10 cm) square. The Luopan is recommended for use in our Feng Shui classes and practice. $50.00 US

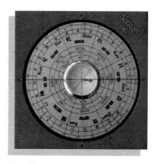

Yi Jing for Love and Marriage

In the journey of life, we often experience times of doubt, confusion and feeling lost. What should we do when facing this type of situation? The Changing Hexagram Divination method can help by prediting what may happen. It can provide guidelines for coping with difficult situations or insight into beneficial ones. This book provides a simple method for the reader to predict the answers to their questions and to help others. Besides resolving confusion and doubt, it also provides a fun hobby for those interested in the ancient art of divination. Use this book as your consultant on Love and Marriage when the need arises! Available in paperback and ebook. $14.75 US

Ten-Thousand Year Calendar (1882 - 2031)

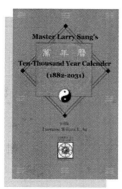

Normally printed in Chinese, but now in English, this handy reference guide is what the Chinese call the Ten-Thousand Year Calendar. This calendar contains information for 150 years, from 1882 to 2031. It gives the annual, monthly, and daily stem and branch, the annual and monthly flying star, as well as the lunar day of the month. It also gives information about the lunar and solar months, the solstices, equinoxes, and the beginning of the four seasons in the Chinese calendar. The Ten-Thousand Year Calendar is used for Feng Shui, Chinese Astrology, Day Selection, and various predictive techniques. 165 Pages.

Available in e-book only. $26.00 US

Feng Shui Facts and Myths

This book is a collection of stories about Feng Shui and Astrology. Master Sang attempts to explain aspects of Feng Shui and Chinese Astrology, as the terms are understood or misunderstood in the West. This book will provide you with deeper information on the Chinese cultural traditions of Feng Shui and Astrology. Available in paperback and ebook.

$16.00 US

Larry Sang's 2009
Chinese Astrology & Feng Shui Guide
The Year of the Ox

Each section explains how to determine the key piece: determining your animal sign; how to read the Feng Shui of your home; and how to read the Day Selection calendar - a valuable day by day indication of favorable and unfavorable activity. Available in paperback and ebook. $14.75 US

COURSE CATALOG

The following is a current list of the courses available from *The American Feng Shui Institute*. Please consult our online catalog for course fees, descriptions and new additions.

FENG SHUI		
CLASS	**CLASS NAME**	**PREREQUISITE**
FS095	Introduction to Feng Shui	-
FS101/OL	Beginning Feng Shui & Online	-
FS102/OL	Intermediate Feng Shui & Online	FS101 or FS101/OL
FS201/OL	Advanced Feng Shui & Online	FS102 or FS102/OL
FS205/OL	Advanced Sitting and Facing & Online	FS102/OL
FS106/OL	Additional concepts on Sitting and Facing	FS201
FS225	Feng Shui Folk Beliefs	FS201
FS227/OL	Professional Skills for Feng Shui Consultants	FS201
FS231	Feng Shui Yourself & Your Business	FS201
FS235	Symptoms of a House	FS201
FS250	Explanation of Advanced Feng Shui Theories	FS201
FS275	9 Palace Grid & Pie Chart Graph Usage	FS201
FS280	Advanced East West Theory	FS201
FS301	Advanced Feng Shui Case Study 1 & 2	FS201
FS303	Advanced Feng Shui Case Study 3 & 4	FS201
FS305/OL	Advanced Feng Shui Case Study 5 & 6	FS201
FS307/OL	Advanced Feng Shui Case Study 7	FS201
FS308/OL	Advanced Feng Shui Case Study 8	FS201
FS309	Advanced Feng Shui Case Study 9 & 10	FS201
FS311	Advanced Feng Shui Case Study 11	FS201
FS312	Advanced Feng Shui Case Study 12	FS201
FS313/OL	Advanced Feng Shui Case Study 13	FS201 & AS101
FS314	Advanced Feng Shui Case Study 14	FS201
FS315	Advanced Feng Shui Case Study 15	FS201
FS316	Advanced Feng Shui Case Study 16 & 17	FS201
FS340/OL	Secrets of the Five Ghosts	FS201
FS341	The Secrets of the "San Ban Gua"	FS201

FENG SHUI - *continued from previous page*		
FS260/OL	Lawsuit Support & Online	FS201 & AS101
FS270/OL	The Taisui, Year Breaker, Three Sha & Online	FS201 & AS101
FS350/OL	Feng Shui Day Selection 1 & Online	FS201 & AS101
FS351/OL	Feng Shui Day Selection 2 & Online	FS350 or FS350OL
FS360/OL	Marriage and Life Partner Selection Online	FS201 & AS101
FS375	Introduction to Yin House Feng Shui	FS201
YI JING		
YJ101	Beginning Yi Jing Divination	AS101
YJ102	Yi Jing Coin Divination	AS101
YJ103	Plum Flower Yi Jing Calculation	AS101
CHINESE ASTROLOGY		
AS101/OL	Stems and Branches & Online	-
AS102	Four Pillars 1 & 2 (Zi Ping Ba Zi)	AS101 or AS101OL
AS103	Four Pillars 3 & 4 (Zi Ping Ba Zi)	AS102
	Four Pillars 5 & 6 (Zi Ping Ba Zi)	AS103
AS201A/OL	Beginning Zi Wei Dou Shu, Part 1	AS101
AS201B/OL	Beginning Zi Wei Dou Shu, Part 2	AS201A/OL
AS211/OL	Intermediate Zi Wei Dou Shu	AS201B/OL
AS301A/OL	Advanced Zi Wei Dou Shu, Part 1	AS211/OL
AS301B/OL	Advanced Zi Wei Dou Shu, Part 2	AS201A/OL
AS311/OL	Zi Wei Dou Shu Case Study 1	AS301B/OL
AS313/OL	Zi Wei Dou Shu Case Study 3	AS301B/OL
	Zi Wei Dou Shu Case Study 2 & 4	
CHINESE ARTS		
CA101/OL	Palm and Face Reading 1 & 2	-
CA102	Palm and Face Reading 3 & 4	CA101 or CA101/OL
CA103	Palm and Face Reading for Health	-
CA121	Introduction to Chinese Medicine	-
CHINESE PHILOSOPHY		
CP101	Introduction to Daode Jing	-
CP102	Feng Shui Yourself	-

Classes at the American Feng Shui Institute:

Due to the limited seating capacity, reservations are necessary and seats are on a first come first serve basis. The reserve your seat, a $50.00 US deposit is required and is non-refundable if cancellation by student takes place less than three days before class. Please mail-in a check or call us to reserve your seat with a credit card*. Balance is due on the first day of class.

Online classes with the American Feng Shui Institute feature:

- Easy navigation
- Self tests at the end of each module
- A discussion board with trained Institute instructors
- Audio clips for pronounciation
- An online discussion board
- An instant feedback final exam

The online classes are self-paced study modules. They are segmented into four, one-week lessons that lead you at your own pace, over the four-week course. You have 60 days to complete the course work.

For more information, please see our website:
www.amfengshui.com

You may register at any time online, or by phone or fax

Tel: 626.571.2757
Fax: 626.281.0042

Email: fsinfo@amfengshui.com

Address:
American Feng Shui Institute
111 N. Atlantic Blvd. Suite 352
Monterey Park, CA 91754

Please DO NOT email credit card information as this is not a secure method

As a Student of the American Feng Shui Institute:

You will receive a certificate of completion from the American Feng Shui Institute, for the Beginning/Intermediate and Advanced Feng Shui Classes. Please do not confuse this certification or licensing, as there are no requirements for practitioner at this time.

As a student of the Institute, we are available to assist you with your studies. We have an online Bulletin Board for questions and answer, featuring a topic search. You will obtain access to the Bulletin Board upon completion of the Advanced Feng Shui class. Due to the complexity of the courses, graduates may repeat in the classroom any class that you have already taken, for $45.00 US per day, pending available seats. Please see our online course catalog for the most current course offerings.

Cancellation and Refund Policy:

All institutional charges shall be returned to the registrant less a $50.00 US cancellation fee, if cancellation notice is received prior to or on the first day of instruction. Any notification of withdrawal or cancellation and any request for a refund are required to be made in writing.

Refunds shall be made within thirty (30) days of receipt of the withdrawal or cancellation notice and refund request.

The institute does not participate in the Student Tuition Recovery Fund (STRF). We are registered with the state of California. Registration means we have met certain minimum standards imposed by the state for registered schools on the basis of our written application to the state. Registration does not mean we have met all of the more extensive standards required by the state for schools that are approved to operate or license or that the state has verified the information we submitted with our registration form.

THANK YOU